A Garland Series

The English Stage
Attack and Defense 1577 - 1730

A collection of 90 important works
reprinted in photo-facsimile in 50 volumes

FLORIDA GULF COAST UNIVERSITY LIBRARY

edited by
Arthur Freeman
Boston University

The Tragedies of the Last Age Consider'd and Examin'd

and

A Short View of Tragedy

by

Thomas Rymer

with a preface
for the Garland Edition by

Arthur Freeman

Garland Publishing, Inc., New York & London

1974

Copyright © 1974

by Garland Publishing, Inc.

All Rights Reserved

PN
1891
.R82
1974

Library of Congress Cataloging in Publication Data

Rymer, Thomas, 1641-1713.
　The tragedies of the last age consider'd and
examin'd, and A short view of tragedy.

　(The English stage: attack and defense, 1577-1730)
　Reprint of 2 works, the 1st printed in 1678 for
R. Tonson, London; the 2d printed and sold in 1693 by
R. Baldwin, London.
　　1. Tragedy--History and criticism.　I. Rymer,
Thomas, 1641-1713.　A short view of tragedy.　1974.
II. Title.　III. Title: A short view of tragedy.
IV. Series.
PN1891.R82　1974　　　　809.2'51　　　　79-170435
ISBN 0-8240-0601-1

Printed in the United States of America

Preface

Thomas Rymer's Short View of Tragedy *has long been a key text in the study of Shakespeare criticism, above all for its vehement censure of* Othello *as "a bloody farce, without salt or savour." But an earlier essay on the classic English drama,* The Tragedies of the Last Age Consider'd and Examin'd, *though it is less specifically centered on Shakespeare, has many claims to our attention — among others that it precedes* A Short View *by fifteen years.*

Tragedies of the Last Age *followed hard on Rymer's failure of a play,* Edgar *(1677); it concentrates its hostile criticism of earlier drama upon three Fletcher or Beaumont and Fletcher plays still in vogue,* Rollo, Duke of Normandy, A King and No King *and* The Maid's Tragedy, *although it announces an intention to deal as well with* Othello, Julius Caesar, *Jonson's* Cataline, *and even* Paradise Lost. *Iconoclastic as he is, and "tyrannical" as Samuel Johnson called him, Rymer's zoilist criticism is not without its force and freshness. We may rarely agree with him, but he provokes us to a thoughtful defense of what are, after all, remarkably successful works of art.*

Tragedies of the Last Age *is dated 1678, but was*

PREFACE

*available in December 1677 (*Term Catalogues, *I, 294). In late 1692 the book was reissued with a cancel title, as "Part I. The Second Edition," conceivably as an* ex post facto *exploitation of* A Short View *(see below), for certainly most of the sheets of the latter "edition" are remainders, rather than what the* Gentleman's Journal *of December 1692 calls it — "being very scarce" and "reprinted, to be bound up with the last [i.e.,* A Short View*]." A last reissue (1694) is known only from a copy in Dr. Williams' Library; one is led to suspect that the book proved hard to sell.*

Not so A Short View of Tragedy, *which attracted positive and antagonistic notice from the time of its issue, by December 1692. Laudatory reviews appeared in that month in John Dunton's* Compleat Library *and, by Peter Motteux, in the* Gentleman's Journal. *It would appear that contemporary readers and critics did not view the two books as "Part I" and "Part II" (cf. the separate listings, both inexplicably as quartos, in the* Term Catalogues *for February 1693, II, 442) but as separate publications, and hence it may seem likely that* The Tragedies of the Last Age *was reissued to capitalize upon the furor attending the reception of* A Short View. *Furthermore, the well-known replies of John Dennis and Charles Gildon to* A Short View *treat it as a separate work.*

There is apparently no modern reprint of Tragedies of the Last Age; *ours is made from the*

PREFACE

1678 first edition, British Museum 641.b.25., collating [ ]⁸B-K⁸ (license leaf and title page supplied from a copy at Yale). The book is edited by Curt A. Zimansky, The Critical Works of Thomas Rymer *(1956), as is* A Short View; *the latter has also been reprinted with a preface by the present editor, from the Stratford copy, by Frank Cass, Ltd. (1970-73). We employ here the Yale University copy (Beinecke Ib 72.i.678b), collating A-M⁸N⁴[A1 blank]. Wing R 2430 and 2429; Lowe-Arnott-Robinson 3697 and 3705.*

February, 1973   A.F.

Licensed,

July 17, 1677.   *R. L'estrange,*

THE
Tragedies
OF
The last Age

Consider'd and Examin'd
BY THE
Practice of the Ancients,
AND BY THE
Common sense of all Ages.
IN A
LETTER
TO
Fleetwood Shepheard, Esq;

By THOMAS RYMER, of
Grays-Inn, Esquire.

―― *Clament periisse pudorem.*
Cuncti pene patres; ea quum reprehendere coner
Quæ gravis Æsopus, quæ doctus Roscius egit. Hor.

London, Printed for *Richard Tonson* at his Shop
under *Grays-Inn* Gate, next *Grays-Inn*
Lane, 1678.

The Contents.

ACtion, the unity *must be obſerv'd, or elſe the conduct will be all at random*, 106.

where the unity is obſerv'd, the Play cannot have two ſeveral Names, 106.

where obſerv'd, the Poet cannot eaſily tranſgreſs in the unities of time and place, 24.

Actors *make the ſucceſs of Plays*, 6. 138.

Ariſtotle *on Poeſie long conn'd in Italy, e're heard of on this ſide of the Alps*, 142.

Argument, Plot *or* Fable *for a Tragedy ought to be taken from Hiſtory*, 17. 56.

ought to be more accurate and Philoſophical

The Contents.

losophical then History, 14. 16.
ought to represent persons better then the life, 36.

Antiochus's *conduct when in love with his stepmother*, 78.

Antigone *of* Sophocles *its Argument*, 40.

Athens *and* London *the same for Nature and Manners*, 6.

Athens *and* Malmsbury *have the same Test for Tragedy*, 99.

Athenians *a fighting people*, 27, 28.

Authors *of* English *Tragedy began not where the Antients left off*, 11.
How they would have Character'd Phedra, 92.

B.

Ben. Johnson *preferr'd*, 144.
Bloodshed rarely on the Antient Theaters, and why, 27, 28.

Canace

The Contents.

C.

Canace Parturiens. Nero *the Emperour an actor in it*, 70.
Canace *of* Speroni Sperone, *its argument and preparation*, 77.
Crime, *when extenuated by the Antients*, 27. 78.

D.

Decorum *shockt*, 37. 39. 42. 47. *and throughout*.

E.

Empericks in Poetry, 5.
English *Language proper for Tragedy*, 10, 11.
Episode *by whom introduc'd*, 12. *gave offence to the Priests*, 12.
Epic Poems and Tragedys *agree*, 74. *differ* 120.

Euri-

The Contents.

Euripides *blamed by the Antients for making Characters more wicked then they should be*, 36.
his Etheocles *and* Polynices, 30, 31, 32. *& ult.*
his Phedra, 79, 80.
Evil design to be represented in its fall but not in its advances, 75, 76.

F.

Fable the soul of a Tragedy, 4. 19.
Fanaticks in Poetry, 8.
Fancy not straitned by rules, 9.
Frailties, Comical and Heroick frailties, 45.

H.

Hart and Mohun *the* Æsopus *and* Roscius *of the English stage.* 138.
Historical and accidental truths will not do in Tragedy, 14, 15, 19, 47.
Historical impudence, 114.

In-

The Contents.

I.

INstinct of good use in Poetry, 64.

K.

Kings are all in Poetry presumptive Heroes, 61.
ridiculously pictur'd, 60.
not to be sway'd by evil Ministers, 46, 47.
profan'd in these Tragedies every where, 107. 114.
cannot be accessary to a crime, 115.
one without a Name, 107.

M.

Madness, what sort to be imitated in Poetry, 80.
Mans life not to be taken away without a just account, 23.
Manners to be reform'd by Poetry, 7.

Me-

The Contents.

Mezentius *made an object of Pity,* 120.

Murders in these Tragedies every where absurd, 120.

P.

*P*Assion *allows no long speeches,* 44. *no comparisons,* 54. *no parenthesis,* 128.

Please, what naturally, 5. 14. *and throughout.*

Pictures how they please, 15.

Poets not incomprehensible, 14.
  must take care that the Criminal sin not too far, and are not to be trusted for an Hell behind the Scenes, 26.
  Not to take Nature at the second hand, 140.
  what the end and design of Poetry, 13, 14, 15. 142.

Poetical Justice, 23. 25, 26. 37. 128.
  poetical death, 42.

Pity and Terror, 25. 27. 28. *and throughout.*

Prepara-

The Contents.

Preparation; what it ought to be for an incestuous love, 79.
What for two Brothers that kill each other, 29, 30, to 36.
What for making a King, 38, 39.
Phedra *in* Euripides; *her love not voluntary*, 79, 80.
Her secrecy, conflict and frenzy, 80.
Her fortitude, 82, 90, 91.
Her ravings, 81.
Her reveres, and good sense, 83.
The Nurses importunity and subtilty, 81.
How ready to catch at the least hint, 82.
Speech to debauch Phedra, *from* 85 *to* 89.
How she equivocates, and deceives Phedra: *and speaks to* Hippolytus *without her consent or privity*, 91, 92.
Phedra *in* Seneca, *the whole conduct unnatural, absurd, nor any way tending to move pitty, or terror*, 93, 94, 95, 96.

Reason

The Contents.

R.

REason is to discipline fancy, 8, 109.

S.

Scene wrought up, if not skilfully, torments nature, 76, 113.
Scene; which only in these Plays proper to move pitty, 132.
But the occasion none of the greatest, the Conduct coarse, the Turn faulty, the Counter-turn ridiculous, 133, 134, 135, 136.
An instance of a Scene with all these in perfection, 137, 138.
Socrates brought moral Philosophy in Vogue, assisted by Sophocles and Euripides, 13.
Seneca his Phedra, 93.
His thoughts often from the purpose, 97.
Speech of Julia in Herodian, 49.
Of Sophia in the Play, 50, 51.

Com-

The Contents.

Compar'd together, 52, 53.
Speeches *of more mettle,* 54, 55.
Speech *of* Cassius *and* Arbaces *compar'd,* 103.

T.

Tragedy, *its reputation in former days,* 2.
What Originally, 11.
Requirrs what is great in nature, 43, 65, 80, 85.
Ours of the last age without design, 16.
Unpolitical, 29.
Of Rollo, *the Argument,* 18.
Condemn'd, 19, 41.
How it ought to have been contriv'd with the same catastrophe, 19, 20.
And how the characters of Rollo, Otto, Aubrey *and* Matilda *ought to have been design'd,* 21, 22, 23.
Rollo *and* Otto *compar'd with* Etheocles *and* Polynices *in* Euripides, *from* 30 *to* 36.
Characters, as we find them, of Rollo, 37.

Of

The Contents.

Of Aubrey, 38.
Of Sophia, 42.
Of Matilda, ib.
Of Edith, 43, 44, 45.
Of Latorch, 46.
Several reasons why Edith *rather than* Hamond *should have kill'd the King*, 47, 48.
Reasons *for the success of this Tragedy*, 55.
A King *and* no King, *the Title Comical*, 57.
The Plot, ib.
Nothing accurate or Philosophical in it, 57, 58, 59.
How the Plot ought to have been cast, 58.
Improbabilities and the characters unlikely, and all unproper, 59.
Character of Arbaces, 61, 62, 63.
What it should have been, 63.
How wisely he acquits himself when un-King'd, 65, 66, 67.
Ought rather to have been knockt o'th head than to have marri'd a Princess, 67.
The Princess is made more silly than any common Shepherdess, 68, 69.

The

The Contents.

The Queen-Mother a Patient Grissei, 70.
Reason of this Tragedy's success, 5.
  Maids Tragedy, its Argument, 104.
  Unnatural, improbable, 106, 107, 113.
  How it might have been better, 126.
  Action double, 106.
The King a fool and mad-man 109.
Evadne a Monster,
Melantius, 122.
Callianax, 123.
Aspatia, 123.
Amintor, 125.

W.

Who and who may kill one another with decency, 117.
Wilful murder not to be suffer'd in Tragedy, 27.
Wicked persons not to be brought on the Stage, 120.
Women judges, 4, 5, 95, 96.
  Modesty necessary and essential to their character, 113.
  Are not to suffer any cruelties from man, 70, 74.

The Contents.

Virgil's *infinite care on that occasion*, 71, 72.

Yet corrected by Varus *and* Tucca, 73.

Advertisement.

There is also to be printed an *Heroick Tragedy*, call'd

EDGAR

By the same Hand.

The ERRATA.

Page 9. l. 12. r. *fates.* p. 12. l. 7. 9. r. *Episode.* p. 44. l. ult. for the first r. *his.* and r. *complements.* p. 54. l. 19. for *matter* r. *mettle.* p. 62. l. 18. for *the* r. *thee.* p. 48. l. 18. r. *knew.* p. 100. l. 12. dele *a.* p. 109. l. 6. for *she* r. *he.* p. 100. l. ult. r. *Evadne's.* p. 112. l. 21. r. *Lady's.* p. 116. l. 15. for *nisi* r. *si.* p. 118. l. 13. r. μῶρος. p. 124. l. 10. r. *with.*

TO
Fleetwood Shepheard, Esq;

Having several mornings, and early, travell'd to St. *James's,* with the only design of being with you; and missing you as often; I became so mortifi'd with the misfortune, that I resolv'd to come into the Town no more, till assur'd of your return from *Copt-Hill*: but because I meant not altogether to kill my self, for my entertainment I provided me some of those *Master pieces* of Wit, so renown'd every-where, and so edifying to the *Stage*: I mean the choicest and most applauded *English Tragedies* of this last age; as *Rollo*; *A King and no King*; the *Maids Tragedy*

gedy by *Beaumont* and *Fletcher:* *Othello*, and *Julius Cæsar*, by *Shakespear*; and *Cataline* by Worthy *Ben*.

These I perus'd with some attention, and some reflections I made; in which, how far I mistake your sense, that is, how far I am mistaken, I desire to be inform'd.

I had heard that the *Theater* was wont to be call'd the *School* of *Vertue*; and *Tragedy* a *Poem* for *Kings*: That they who first brought Tragedy to perfection, were made *Vice-Roys* and Governors of *Islands*; were honoured every-where with Statues of Marble, and Statues of Brass; were stil'd the *Wise Sophocles*, the *Wise Euripides* by God and Man, by Oracles and Philosophers. That for teaching Morality, *Crantor* and *Chrysippus* were no-body to 'em. This latter transcrib'd the whole *Medea* of *Euripides* into his works. That so refin'd a People, and so frugal a *Common-wealth* as *Athens* did tax and assess themselves, and laid out more of their publick Exchequer upon the representation of these Plays, than all
their

their Wars stood them in, though sometimes both Seas and Land were cover'd with Pagan Enemies that invaded them. And not *Athens* only, but (who hated *Athens*) so austere and glum a generation as those of *Sparta*, by the care of *Lycurgus*, agreed the same honour to these *Athenian Poets*.

These things coming into my mind, surely (thought I) mens brains lye not in the same place as formerly; or else Poetry is not now the same thing it was in those days of yore.

I therefore made enquiry what *difference* might be in our *Philosophy* and *Manners*; I found that our *Philosophers* agreed well enough with theirs, in the *main*; however, that our Poets have forc'd another way to the *wood*; a *by-road*, that runs directly cross to that of *Nature*, *Manners* and *Philosophy* which gain'd the *Ancients* so great veneration.

I would not examin the *proportions*, the *unities* and *outward* regularities, the *mechanical part* of Tragedies: there is no talking of Beauties

ties when there wants Essentials; 'tis not necessary for a man to have a nose on his face, nor to have two legs: he may be a *true* man, though aukward and unsightly, as the *Monster* in the *Tempest*.

Nor have I much troubl'd their phrase and expression, I have not vex'd their language with the *doubts*, the *remarks* and eternal triflings of the *French Grammaticasters*: much less have I cast about for Jests, and gone a quibble-catching.

I have chiefly consider'd the *Fable* or *Plot*, which all conclude to be the *Soul* of a *Tragedy*; which, with the *Ancients*, is always found to be a *reasonable Soul*; but *with us*, for the most part, a *brutish*, and often worse than *brutish*.

And certainly there is not requir'd much Learning, or that a man must be some *Aristotle*, and *Doctor* of *Subtilties*, to form a right judgment in this particular; common sense suffices; and rarely have I known the *Women-judges* mistake in these points, when they have the patience to think,
and

and (left to their own heads) they decide with their own sense. But if people are prepossest, if they will judg of *Rollo* by *Othello*, and one *crooked line* by another, we can never have a certainty.

Amongst those who will be objecting against the doctrin I lay down, may peradventure appear a sort of men who have remember'd *so* and *so*; and value themselves upon their *experience*. I may write by the *Book* (say they) what I have a mind, but they *know* what will *please*. These are a kind of *Stage-quacks* and *Empericks* in Poetry, who have got a *Receit* to *please*: And no *Collegiate* like 'em for *purging* the Passions.

These say (for instance) a *King* and no *King, pleases*. I say the *Comical* part *pleases*.

I say that Mr. *Hart pleases*; most of the business falls to his share, and what he *delivers*, every one takes upon *content*; their *eyes* are prepossest and charm'd by his *action*, before ought of the *Poets* can approach their *ears*; and to the most wretched of *Characters*, he gives a lustre and *brillant* which dazles the *sight*, that the *deformities* in the Poetry cannot be perceiv'd.

Therefore a distinction is to be made between what *pleases naturally* in it self, and what *pleases* upon the account of *Machines*, *Actors*, *Dances* and circumstances which are meerly *accidental* to the *Tragedy*.

Aristotle observes, that in his time, some who (wanting the talent to *write* what might *please*) made it their care that the *Actors* should help out, where the *Muses* faild.

These objectors urge, that there is also another great *accident*, which is, that *Athens* and *London* have not the same *Meridian*.

Certain it is, that *Nature* is the same, and *Man* is the same, he *loves*, *grieves*, *hates*, *envies*, has the same *affections* aud *passions* in both places, and the same *springs* that give them *motion*. What mov'd *pity* there, will *here* also produce the same effect.

This must be confest, unless they will, in effect say, that we have not

that

that *delicate taſt* of things; we are not ſo *refin'd*, nor ſo *vertuous*; that *Athens* was more *civiliz'd* by their *Philoſophers*, than we with both our *Philoſophers* and *twelve Apoſtles*.

But were it to be ſuppos'd that *Nature* with us is a *corrupt* and deprav'd *Nature*, that we are *Barbarians*, and *humanity* dwells not amongſt us; ſhall our *Poet* therefore pamper this *corrupt* nature, and indulge our barbarity? Shall he not rather *purge* away the corruption, and reform our *manners*? Shall he not with *Orpheus* rather chooſe to draw the *Brutes* after him, than be himſelf a *follower* of the *Herd*? Was it thus that the *ancient* Poets (by the beſt Philoſophers) became ſtil'd the *Fathers* of Knowledg, and *Interpreters* of the Gods?

Laſtly, (though *Tragedy* is a Poem chiefly for *men* of *ſenſe*,) yet I cannot be perſwaded that the people are ſo very mad of *Acorns*, but that they could be well content to eat the *Bread* of civil perſons.

Say others, *Poetry* and *Reason*, how come these to be Cater-cousins? Poetry is the *Child* of *Fancy*, and is never to be school'd and *disciplin'd* by *Reason*; Poetry, say they, is *blind* inspiration, is pure *enthusiasm*, is *rapture* and *rage* all over.

But *Fancy*, I think, in Poetry, is like *Faith* in Religion; it makes far discoveries, and soars above reason, but never clashes, or runs against it. *Fancy* leaps, and frisks, and away she's gone; whilst *reason* rattles the chains, and follows after. *Reason* must consent and ratify what-ever by *fancy* is attempted in its absence; or else 'tis all *null* and void in law. However, in the contrivance and *œconomy* of a Play, *reason* is always principally to be consulted. Those who object against reason, are the *Fanaticks* in Poetry, and are never to be sav'd by their good works.

Others imagin that these rules and restraints on the *Plot* and *Argument* of Tragedy, wou'd hinder much good *intrigue*, wou'd clog invention, and make all *Plays* alike and *uniform*.

But

But certainly *Nature* affords plenty and variety enough of *Beauties*, that no man need complain if the *deform'd* are cloyster'd up, and shut from him. Such a Painter has been, who could draw nothing but a *Rose*; yet other Painters can design one and the same good face in a thousand several figures: it may be remember'd that there are but five vowels; or be considered, from *seven* Planets, and their several positions, how *many fates* and fortunes the *Astrologer* distributes to the people. And has not a Poet more *vertues* and *vices* within his *circle*, cannot he observe them and their influences in their several *situations*, in their *oppositions* and *conjunctions*, in their *altitudes* and *depressions*: and he shall sooner find his *ink*, than the *Stores* of Nature exhausted.

Other objections may be answer'd as they fall in the way. I would only have you before hand advertiz'd, that you will find me ty'd to no certain *stile*, nor laying my reasons together in *form* and *method*. You will find me sometimes reasoning, sometimes

times declaiming, sometimes citing authority for common sense; sometimes *uttering*, as my *own*, what may be had at any *Bookshop* in the Nation: sometimes doubting when I might be positive, and sometimes confident out of season; sometimes turning *Tragedy* into what is *light* and comical, and sporting when I should be serious. This variety made the travel more easy. And you know I am not cut out for writing a *Treatise*, nor have a *genius* to *pen* any thing *exactly*; so long as I am *true* to the *main sense* before me, you will pardon me in the rest.

Nor will it, I hope, give offence that I handle these *Tragedies* with the same liberty that I formerly had taken in examining the *Epick Poems* of *Spencer*, *Cowley*, and such names as will ever be *sacred* to me. *Rapin* tells us, for his own *Countreymen*, that none of them had writ a good *Tragedy*, nor was ever like to write one. And an (*a*) eminent Ita-

(*a*) *O sia stata la loro poca fortuna, ò l'imperferione della nostra lingua nelle cose gravi e A. Tassone.*

lian

lian confesses, that the best of theirs exceeded not a mediocrity; and yet their *Divine Tasso* had then writ a Tragedy, and *Torrismodo* strutted it in *buskins*.

But I have elsewhere declar'd my opinion, that the *English* want neither *genius* nor *language* for so great a work. And, certainly, had our Authors began with Tragedy, as *Sophocles* and *Euripides* left it; had they either built on the same foundation, or after their *model*; we might e're this day have seen Poetry in greater perfection, and boasted such *Monuments* of wit as *Greece* or *Rome* never knew in all their *glory*.

According to the best account I can gather from old Authors. Tragedy was originally, with the Ancients, a piece of *Religious* worship, a part of their *Liturgy*. The Priests sung an Anthem to their god *Diony-*

Dionysus, whilst the *Goat* (*b*) stood at his Altar to be *sacrific'd:* And this was call'd the *Goat-song* or *Tragedy*.

These Priests were call'd the *Chorus*, and now the whole Ceremony was perform'd by them, till *Thespis* introduc'd the *Episods*, and brought an *Actor* on the Stage.

Which *Episods* the Priests at first mutini'd against as an *Innovation*, they listen'd a long while, thought it ran off from the Text, and wonder'd how it wou'd be appli'd, till at last their patience could hold no longer, and they roar'd out, (*c*) *Nothing to* Dionisus, *nothing to* Dionysus, which gave beginning to the Proverb.

But the *Poet* gaining upon them by little and little, enlarged the *Episod*, till it grew the *main part;* the *part* which only is by us call'd the

---

(*b*) *Wou'd therefore read in* Horace, Vilem certavit ad hircum, *as*--Rhetor dicturus ad aras; *not being satisfied in Antiquity with what the Commentators devise, when they read,*--- Vilem certavit ob hircum.

(*c*) οὐδὲν πρὸς Διόνυσον.

Tra-

Tragedy. And to make amends to *Dionysus*, the *Theaters* were all consecrated to him, and the Plays acted there, call'd *Dionysus's Plays*.

After much new-modelling, many changes and alterations, *Æschylus* came with a *second* Actor on the Stage, and lessen'd the business of the *Chorus* proportionably. But *Sophocles* adding a *third* Actor, and *painted* Scenes, gave (in *Aristotle's* opinion,) the utmost *perfection* to Tragedy.

And now it was that (the *men* of *sense* grown weary with discoursing of *Atoms* and *empty Space*, and the *humour* of *Mechanical* Philosophy near spent.) *Socrates* set up for *Morality*, and all the buz in *Athens* was now about vertue and good life.

Camerades with him, and Confederates in his worthy design, were our *Sophocles* and *Euripides*: But these took a different method.

He instructed in a pleasant facetious manner, by witty *questions, allusions* and *parables*.

These were for teaching by *examples,*

ples, in a graver way, yet extremely *pleasant* and *delightful*. And, finding in Histoty, the same *end* happen to the *righteous* and to the *unjust*, *vertue* often opprest, and *wickedness* on the Throne: they saw these particular *yesterday-truths* were imperfect and unproper to illustrate the *universal* and *eternal truths* by them intended. Finding also that this *unequal* distribution of rewards and punishments did perplex the *wisest*, and by the *Atheist* was made a scandal to the *Divine Providence*. They concluded, that a *Poet* must of necessity see *justice* exactly administred, if he intended to please. For, said they, if the World can scarce be satisfi'd with God Almighty, whose holy will and purposes are not to be *comprehended*; a *Poet* (in these matters) shall never be pardon'd, who (they are sure) is not *incomprehensible*; whose *ways* and *walks* may, without *impiety*, be penetrated and examin'd. They knew indeed, that many things naturally unpleasant to the World in *themselves*, yet gave *delight* when well
imita-

imitated. These they consider'd as the *(d)* picture of some *deform'd* old Woman, that might cause *laughter*, or some light, superficial, and *comical* pleasure; but never to be endur'd on serious occasions, where the attention of the mind, and where the heart was engaged.

We have pictures that yield another sort of pleasure, as the *last Judgment*, of *Mich. Angelo*, the *Massacre* of the *Innocents*, the *Baptist's* head, &c.

'Tis true; but if they yield any pleasure besides what proceeds from the art, and what rests in eye. 'Tis by the History, to which the picture serves only as an *Index*.

For till our memory goes back to the History, the *head* of the *Baptist* can say no more to us, than the *head* of *Goliah*. But the Ancients in their Tragedies rested not on History.

They found that *History*, grosly taken, was neither proper to *instruct*, nor apt to *please*; and therefore they

(d) Aristotle, *Poet*.

would

would not trust History for their examples, but refin'd upon the History; and thence contriv'd something *(e)* more *philosophical*, and more *accurate* than *History*. But whether our *English* Authors of Tragedy lay their foundation so deep, whether they had any *design* in their *designs*; and whether it was to *prudence* or to *chance* that they sacrific'd, is the business of this present enquiry.

We have in *Herodian* the horrid and bloody story of the two Brothers, *Antoninus* and *Geta*, Emperors, all which (*crude* and undigested, as in the *Original*) we find cram'd into

The Tragedy of Rollo *Duke of* Normandy.

NO reason, I presume, can be given, why, having found an *History*, this Author should change the names; of *Antoninus* and *Geta*

(e) Σπουδαιότερον και φιλοσοφικώτερον.

into

into *Rollo* and *Otto*; *Emperors* of *Rome*, into *Dukes* of *Normandy*. Nor why he alter'd the *Scene* to bring these Cut-throats and *Poisoners* from the other side of the *Alps*. *Aristotle* tells it as extraordinary, of a *Tragedy* made by *Polemon*; wherein both the *names* and *matter* were of his own *invention*; and yet it had the fortune to *please*. He also reminds us that a man is better *pleas'd* with the *picture* of an *acquaintance*, than of a person of whom we had never *heard*. And we generally observe, when one tells of an *adventure*, or but a jeast, he will choose to father it on some one that is *known*, thereby to get attention, and gain more credit to what he relates. Besides, many things are *probable* of *Antoninus*, or of *Alexander*, and *particular* men, because they are *true*, which cannot be *generally probable*: and he that will be *feigning* persons, should confine his fancy to *general probability*.

The Fable is this:

Rollo and *Otto* Brothers, and both equally (let me call them) Kings of one and the same Kingdom, cannot agree about the matter. *Rollo* (by the means of his favourite *Latorch*) attempts to poison his Brother; which failing, he kills *Otto* in the arms of their Mother *Sophia*, with Sword drawn offers to kill his Mother and Sister *Mat.* but is disarm'd by *Aubrey*, yet sends out Lord Chancellor *Gisbert* to be chopt in two, and thrown to the dogs; and his Tutor *Baldwin* also to be beheaded. *Hamond*, Captain of the Guards, saw all this executed. *Allan*, the Captain's Brother gives (his *quondam-*Master) the Chancellor, Christian Burial: for which, he is sent to pot. *Edith*, *Baldwin*'s Daughter, beseeches the King to spare her Father; prevails, but too late. *Rollo* is in love with her; she resolves his death. *Hamond*, in revenge of his Brother *Allan*, stabs, and is stab'd by *Rollo*, whose
Sister

Sister *Matilda*, *Aubrey* takes to Wife; and Reigns in his stead.

Now, if you call this a Fable; give me one of old *Æsop*'s; where, for all the coarse out-side, there dwells a little *reasonable Soul* within, a little *good Sense* at the bottom, which carries it through all Nations, and will commend it to the end of the World,

For nothing certainly is design'd in this of *Rollo*, either to move *pitty or terror*, either to *delight* or *instruct*.

It is indeed a History, and it may well be a History; for never man of common *sense* could set himself to invent any thing so gross.

Poetry requires the *ben trovato*, something *handsomely invented*, and leaves the *truth* to History; but never were the Muses profan'd with a more foul, unpleasant, and unwholsome *truth*, than this which makes the Argument of *Rollo*.

If the *end* of this *Tragedy* is the Marriage and Coronation of *Aubrey*, had one of the ancient Poets been to cultivate this History; They would have laid the right of the Crown in
Aubrey.

Aubrey. They would have given us to understand, that *Aubrey*'s Father, a good King, rais'd *Rollo*'s Father from a mean condition to be his favourite, and have the places of greatest trust and confidence with him. This ungrateful Villain most treacherously murders the King his Master, settles himself on his Throne, dies in Peace, leaves the Kingdom equally to his two Sons. These Sons enter upon the Government, the people swear Allegiance to 'em, Complement them with Addresses from all Countreys; the Air rings with *Vive-le-Roy's* and Acclamations. The Sun shines as it was wont, the Grass grows, Cows give white Milk, and no *Ægyptian* Plague troubles the Land. Heaven has forgot, and human means appear none, for either revenging the murder'd King, or restoring his Son *Aubrey*.

Now is the time for a Poet to shew his cunning. Now he must bring a sudden and terrible judgment to destroy the *Rollian*-Race, and set young *Aubrey* on the Throne of his Ancestors. To

To effect this, the two Brothers must be made to kill each other; and, as a consequence of this disaster, their Mother is to kill her self for sorrow.

These Brothers, in their character, would have been harmless men, modest enough, and loving each other tenderly: for had they been wicked, the judgment upon them might be apply'd as due to their own crimes. Or however their Fathers crime in it self would have appear'd less, as not enough alone to deserve that vengeance; and if the occasion was not clear, the punishment would be less regarded; but their innocence makes the punishment more signal and extraordinary, and more discovers the work of Heaven. And thus also they are capable of moving pitty, when only their Father's crime pursues them; and it seems likely that, otherwise, they might have liv'd happily together.

Their Sister *Matilda* must have been a vertuous sweet Lady, every way of singular merit, sensible of her

Father's crime, and of the wrong that *Aubrey* suffers. By this character, all those who had *pittied* her Brothers, would have been extremely satisfi'd to see their Sister so well preferr'd in the Marriage with *Aubrey*; for Heaven, by this, would seem, in her, to make some amends for the hard measure to the unfortunate Brothers.

Aubrey should in all his words and actions appear great, promising, and Kingly, to deserve that care which Heaven manifests so wonderfully in his Restoration.

And because this, of the two Brothers killing each other, is an action *morally* unnatural; therefore, by way of *preparation*, the *Tragedy* would have begun with Heaven and Earth in disorder, *nature* troubl'd, unheard-of *prodigies*; something (if I may so say) *physically* unnatural, and against the ordinary course of nature. Perhaps the first *Scene* would have shew'd the Usurper's *Ghost* from Hell, full of horror for his crime, cursing his Sons, and sending some infernal *fury* amongst them.   And.

And, by the way, he might relate all things fit to be known, which paſt out of the *Drama*.

The nicety in writing upon this *Fable*, would have chiefly been in the *characters* of the two Brothers, Theſe are the perſons kill'd, and, of all things, a Poet muſt be tender of a mans life, and never *ſacrifice* it to his *Maggot* and *Capriccio*. Therefore, as (I ſaid) the Brothers were not to be *wicked*, ſo likewiſe they ought not to be abſolutely innocent. For if they had refuſed to ſucceed their Father, and when they might have ſat on the Throne, have humbled themſelves at *Aubrey*'s feet; then no *Poetical Juſtice* could have touch'd them : guilty they were to be, in enjoying their Father's crime; but not of committing any new. And this guilt of theirs was alſo either to be palliated, or elſe to be paſt over in ſilence, leſt, laid too open, the compaſſion of the Audience might be abated. Neither would it ſuffice that theſe Brothers kill each other by ſome chance; but it ſhould appear, that agitated by their

Fathers

Father's crime, like *Machines*, they unavoidably clash against each other; whilst their proper *inclination* in vain strives against the *violence*.

If the *English Theatre* requires more *intrigue*, an Author may multiply the *Incidents*, may add *Episods*, and *thicken* the *Plot*, as he sees occasion; provided that all the *lines* tend to the same *center*: more of a main *Plot*, *Virgil* requir'd not for his *Epic* Poem.

And peradventure, if the Poet design any certain *sense* by his *Fable*, that sense will bind him to the *unity of action*; and the *unity* of *action* cannot well exceed the rule for *time*. And these two *unities* will not permit that the Poet can far transgress in the *third*. So that all the *regularities* seem in a manner to be link'd together: but begin with an absurdity, and nothing reasonable can ever follow. If a Pilot puts to Sea without resolving for what Port, none can wonder that he sails not by the *Compass*.

To return to this *Tragedy* of *Rollo*, if

if the stress of the design rests not on *Aubrey*; but the sense of all *terminates* in *Rollo*. The sense must be this; *He that sheds the blood of man, by man shall his blood be shed.* And if this be all, where's the Wonder? Have we not every day cried in the Streets, instances of God's *revenge* against *murder*, more extraordinary, and more poetical than all this comes to? If this be Poetry, *Tyburn* is a better and more ingenious *School* of *Vertue*, than the *Theatre*.

In former times *Poetry* was another thing than *History*, or than the *Law* of the Land. *Poetry* discover'd crimes, the *Law* could never find out; and punish'd those the *Law* had acquitted. The *Areopagus* clear'd *Orestes*, but with what *Furies* did the *Poets* haunt and torment him? and what a wretch made they of *Oedipus*, when the *Casuist* excus'd his *invincible* ignorance?

The *Poets* consider'd, that naturally men were affected with *pitty*, when they saw others suffer more than their fault deserv'd; and *vice*, they thought,

thought, could never be painted too ugly and frightful; therefore, whether they would move *pitty*, or make *vice* detested, it concern'd them to be somewhat of the severest in the punishments they inflicted. Now, because their hands were tied, that they could not punish beyond such a degree; they were oblig'd to have a strict eye on their Malefactor, that he transgrest not too far, that he committed not *two* crimes, when but responsible for *one* : nor, indeed, be so far guilty, as by the Law to deserve death. For though *historical Justice* might rest there; yet *poetical Justice* could not be so content. It would require that the satisfaction be compleat and full; e're the *Malefactor* goes off the *Stage*, and nothing left to God Almighty, and another World. Nor will it suffer that the Spectators trust the *Poet* for a *Hell* behind the *Scenes*; the fire must roar in the conscience of the *Criminal*, the *fiends* and *furies* be conjur'd up to their faces, with a world of *machine* and horrid spectacles; and yet the *Criminal*
could

could never move *pitty*. Therefore amongst the *Ancients* we find no Malefactors of this kind; a wilful Murderer is with them as strange and unknown, as a *Paricide* to the old *Romans*. Yet need we not fancy that they were squeamish, or unacquainted with any of these great *lumping* crimes in that age; when we remember their *Oedipus*, *Orestes*, or *Medea*. But they took care to wash the Viper, to cleanse away the venom, and with such art to prepare the morsel: they made it all Junket to the tast, and all Physick in the operation.

They so qualifi'd, so allaid, and cover'd the *crime* with circumstances, that little could appear on the *Stage*, but either the causes and provocations before it, or the remorse and penitence, the despairs and horrors of conscience which follow'd, to make the *Criminal* every way a fit object for *pitty*. Nor can we imagin their Stage so rarely endur'd any bloodshed, and that the sight was displeasing, because the Spectators were some sort of effeminate, unfighting fel-

fellows. When we remember the Battels of *Marathon* and *Salamin*; and with what small number these very Spectators had routed *Xerxes* and the greatest Armies in the World. For now it was that the *arms* of the *Athenians* (as well as their *arts*) shin'd in their greatest glory.

The truth is, the *Poets* were to move pitty; and this pitty was to be mov'd for the living, who remain'd; and not for the dead. And they found in nature, that men could not so easily pardon a crime committed before their faces; and consequently could not be so easily dispos'd to bestow that pitty on the *Criminal* which the Poets labour'd for. The Poets, I say, found that the sight of the fact made so strong an impression, as no art of theirs could afterwards fully conquer.

But leave reasoning, and return to *Rollo*; it seems very odd to see the first four *Scenes* pass as if nothing extraordinary were towards, without any preparation; and immediately, without more ado, the two Brothers,
two

two Kings, are a fighting. The *Ancients* would have made the Earth tremble, and the Sun start out of the Firmament at a sight so unnatural. Yet we make no more of them, but turn them out, like two Cocks of the Game, for the diversion of the Rabble.

Some have remark'd, that *Athens* being a *Democracy*, the Poets, in favour of their Government, expos'd Kings, and made them unfortunate. But certainly, examin the Kings of their *Tragedies*, they appear all *Heroes*, and ours but *Dogs*, in comparison of them. So respectful they seem to Kings in their *Democracy*, and so unthinking and unpolitick are our *Poets* under a *Monarchy*. *Thebes* was always enemy to *Athens*, yet would not any *National* pique, nor other, provoke the Poets to treat those Kings unhandsomly; because by their rules to have lessen'd the Kings, would have made their *Tragedies* of no effect, in moving the pitty intended by them. They made the Kings *unfortunate*, we make them
wicked

wicked: they made them to be *pittied*, we make them to be *curst* and *abhorr'd*.

That I may, in all hitherto laid down, be the better understood, let it be observ'd what measures *Euripides* took in the Tragedy of *Etheocles* and *Polynices*.

This instance I choose, the condition of those *Theban* Kings being the neerest to this of *Rollo* and *Otto*: for they also were equally Kings, could not agree, kill'd each other. That we might not suspect that the dissention between them rose from any malice of their own, we are let to know, that the Gods owe a vengeance to *Thebes*, which is now ripe, and ready to fall upon them, for a crime of their Founder *Cadmus*.

That their Grandfather *Laius* warn'd by the *Oracle* not to marry, his Marriage had so incens'd the Gods, that now they were punishing his disobedience on the third generation.

That their Father *Oedipus* had curst them, and praid they might dye by each others hands. These

(31)

These Brothers, to avoid their Father's *curse*, agree, not to live together, but to Reign by the year alternately, and each to be King in his turn. According to this agreement, the younger Brother goes into banishment, where he marries, makes Allies of some *hot-headed* Princes, as *Tydeus*, *Capaneus*, and five more, and brings a Confederate Army before *Thebes*. The Brothers have an enterview; *Polynices* demands his *turn*; *Eteocles* answers to this effect.

Now, whilst I may continue a King, I cannot willingly yield to become a Servant. Neither take you a right course, coming with force of Arms, and laying the Countrey wast. Thebes would blush, should I resign my Scepter for fear of the Mycenæan *spears. In fine, Brother, if I am to transgress, for a Kingdom I would transgress; in all the rest* (f) *serve God.*

This haughty speech of *Eteocles* turns all the current of pitty to his Brother's side. Now the Confederates

(f) ἰουβῖνι

fall

fall on to storm the Town, are repuls'd, with great slaughter on both sides. *Etheocles*, notwithstanding he was the King in possession, notwithstanding he knew (by *Tyresias* the Prophet) that the *Thebans* would be *victorious*, and notwithstanding the danger of his Father's *curse*; yet out of his generosity and humanity to save the effusion of innocent blood; offers the single Combat with his Brother; which accepted, both are kill'd, and dye friends. *Etheocles* could not speak, indeed, but his sighs were all tenderness. The last breath of *Polynices* made these words;

(g) *My friend turn'd enemy, but still my friend.*

But though *Polynices* seems ill treated, and his Brother is much too sharp upon him. The reason given by the *Poet*, is, because he brings forreign Forces to invade his *Native Countrey*: and perhaps the Poet on this occasion might somewhat strain his *Philosophy* to gratify the *Politi-*

(g) ὁ φίλος γὰρ ἐχθρὸς ἐγένετ', ἀλλ' ὅμως φίλος

tian.

rian, but the Poet seems so afraid that the *Audience* should forget that these dissentions are the effect of their Ancestors crimes; and in no wise spring from their own ill mind and election; that he is every where a hinting to us the curse entailed on the Family by their Grandfathers Marriage; the violence of superior powers, of Demons and Furies, which we want language to express;
—ἢ δυνά τις ἐεις Θεὸς: or some terrible goddess discord.

—εἴϊ' ἔρις, εἴτε πατὴρ ὁ σὸς αἴτι۞.
εἴτε τὸ δαιμόνιον:—— Whether discord or your Father is the cause, or some ill spirit. Κάδμε παλαιῶν suffer for the old pique against *Cadmus*, νοσεῖ γὸ ἥδε γῆ— the land is sick, ἐκ δ' ἔπνευσ' αὐτοῖς ἀρὰς δεινάς—— breath'd terrible curses against them, ἀρὰς ἀρᾶται παισὶν ἀνοσιωτάταις did curse most unhallowed curses to his Sons, τὰς σὰς ἀρας δ' ἔοικεν ἐκπλησεῖν Θεὸς ἐξ ὧ τεκνῶθη Λάϊ۞ βία Θεῶν. God is ready to fulfil your curses, because in spight of the gods *Laius* made Children, ἀρὰς παραλαβὼν Λάϊς καὶ παισὶ δὲς, handing the curses from *Laius* down to

D his

his posterity, —— ὖ γδ —— ἄνευ Θεῶν τῶ, ——
I was not born such a fool to pull out my own eyes, and curse my Sons, if some of the Gods had not made me mad, says *Oedipus*, διὰ ἢ τὰς ἀλάςορας, —— because of your fiends. ὅ σὸς ἀλάςωρ, —— your fiend is the cause.

ὅθεν ἐπέσσυτο τάνδε γᾶν ἁρπαγαῖσι δαιμόνων τις ἄτα, some bane sent upon the land by evil spirits, γάμων ἐπακτὰν ἄταν, the bane fixed to the Marriage of *Laius*, πατρὸς ὐ φύξεσθ᾽ ἐριννῦς. not escape their Fathers *Furies*, χάρματ᾽ ἐριννύ⊙, the joy of the *Furies*, ἕνεκεν ἐριννύων, because of the *Furies*, πημονὰν ἐριννύων, the Plague of the *Furies*, ςενάζων ἀρὰς τέκνοις, sighing curses against his Sons, καὶ τὸ Θεόθεν, —— what comes from god, δαιμονῶντας, haunted with evil spirits θείᾳ προνοίᾳ νεικέων ἐπώνυμον, *Polynices* had his name from Contention.

By what I have noted one might think the Poet would have us believe that all the Furies in Hell were broke loose and at work to make these two Brothers miserable, and consequently would have us take their

their part, would engage our affections, and carry our heart along with a sense of their sufferings: Heaven and Earth conspire their ruine.

Quid meus Æneas *in te committere tantum*?

What had they done to deserve this persecution? the curse of their Father lay nearest them, and is most insisted on by the Poet, how had they vexed their Father? their Father transported with the sense of his own horrible misfortunes, tore out his own Eyes, and in that condition would have run about the streets, but these two Sons of his kept him within doors by force, this enrag'd him the more, and he threw his curses about him, which some evil spirits (who haunted the house for some old accounts) gladly lay hold on, and never rested till those curses had their effect.

By what has been observ'd any one may judge whether these *Characters* of *Etheocles* and *Polynices*, or those of *Rollo* and *Otto* be the better contrived for moving that pity which
D 2 *Tragedy*

Tragedy requires. And I have been the more particular, becauſe not only *Rollo*, but moſt of the *Characters* in our Tragedies of the laſt Age, may be examin'd by the ſame reaſon. And yet *Eurypides* has been blam'd for making his Characters more *wicked* then they ought to be in *Tragedy* : he was not taxed by *Ariſtophanes* and *Ariſtotle* only, but by *Sophocles*, and the general ſenſe of *Athens* was againſt him. They ſaid, in thoſe days, that Comedy (whoſe Province was humor and ridiculous matter only) was to repreſent things worſe then the truth. Hiſtory to deſcribe the truth, but Tragedy was to invent things better then the truth. Like good Painters they muſt deſign their Images like the Life, but yet better and more beautiful then the Life. The Malefactor of Tragedy muſt be a better ſort of Malefactor then thoſe that live in the preſent Age. For an obdurate impudent, and impenitent Malefactor can neither move compaſſion nor terror ; nor be of any imaginable uſe in *Tragedy*.

See

See we then *Rollo*, fighting with his own Brother and King, equal to himself, and attempting to poyson him, without any remorse; killing him in their mothers arms, without any provocation; calling the Queen their Mother *Belldam*, and with drawn sword threatning to kill both her and his Sister, without any sense of honour or piety; and must we not imagine a Legion of Devils in his belly. When *Rollo* has murder'd his Brother, he stands condemn'd by the Laws of Poetry; and nothing remains but that the Poet see him executed, and the Poet is to answer for all the mischief committed afterwards. But *Rollo* we find has made his escape, and wo be to the Chancellor, to the Schoolmaster, and the Chancellors Man; for those are to be men of this world no longer. Here is like to be *Poetical Justice*, so many lives taken away, and but the life of one guilty person to answer for all, and is not this a strange method of killing? If the *Planets* had contriv'd him for a *Cock* of thirteen, his first Victory should not have been

been the moſt important, he ſhould firſt have praictis'd on his ſubjects, and have riſen by degrees to the height of iniquity. His Brother Soveraign was his top-murder; nothing remain'd after that, unleſs it were his Lady-Mother.

Neither is *Otto* here a much more taking Gentleman, nothing appears in his *Cue* to move pity, or any way make the Audience of his party.

But of all the world who would ever have expected that *Aubrey* is to ſucceed in the Kingſhip? 'Tis a good man, but the dulleſt good man that ever Poet advanc'd to a Throne by ſuch extraordinary means. Some Dreams or old Propheſie ſhould have begun an expectation in us; or ſome *Lambent-fires* incircling his head, have drawn the peoples eyes upon him. *Rollo* and *Otto* muſt both make untimely ends, to make way for *Aubrey*. So ſtrange a Revolution never happens in Poetry, but either Heaven or Earth gives ſome forenotice of it.

However

However, something shining and extraordinary ought to have appear'd in his *Character*. Indeed he parts *Rollo* and *Otto* fighting, and *Rollo* was once disarm'd by him. But then for decencies sake and *Rollo's* credit, he should have been lookt on as something more then a meer Subject. In all the rest he appears an humble endeavourer, speaks honestly to no purpose, is brav'd and abus'd by Rascals. Whereas each step of his shou'd have been attended with such awe and Majesty, that the spectators, if not guess, might at least wish to see him their Soveraign; and have the pleasure to see their wishes successful.

Gisbert and *Baldwin*, Chancellor and Tutor are *Devota Capita*, only come on the *Stage* to make *Rollo* the greater sinner by their murder.

Further to shew his rage against the Chancellor, says *Rollo*,

Captain, besides remember this in chief,
That being executed, you deny,

To

To all his Friends the rites of Funeral,
And cast his Carkass out to Dogs and Fowls.

No reason here is given for this inhumanity.

On the like occasion *Sophocles* contriv'd a Tragedy, the *Plot* is this. By the death of *Etheocles* and *Polynices*, *Creon* King of *Thebes* made an Edict, that none, upon pain of being buried alive, should presume to give burial to *Polynices*, the reasons pretended are, That *Polynices* had brought Forreigners to invade his Country, and *Etheocles* had dyed in his Countreys defence, and therefore it would be unjust to give to both the same honour of Funeral. He further alledges a charge left by *Etheocles* to the same effect. Now the piety of *Antigone* could not digest so hard a Law, but in the night she goes and covers her Brother with earth, is taken by the Watch, and (*Creon* being deaf to all intercession) is sent to punishment. When the Bishop *Tyresias* reproving *Creon* strikes him with remorse,

morse, who thereupon runs himself to reprieve her, hears from her Tomb the last groans of his only Son *Hæmon*, who he finds had stabb'd himself and lay a dying at the feet of *Antigone*, his dead Mistress. This disaster brought the same violent Fate on the Queen *Eurydice*, and with her depriv'd *Creon* of all that could be dear to him in the world.

In this we have every thing *just*, every thing *surprizing*, every thing *passionate* to extremity.

Whereas in *Rollo* we meet with so much stuff lumberd together, that not the least spring can work, nor the least passion stir, that is pleasant or generous; nor the least proportion or beauty of Tragedy appear. *Aristotle* says that an Image drawn with Chalk in the exact shape and symmetry, will please more then a whole potful of the best Colours thrown upon a wall without any figure or design.

But to proceed with the Characterrs. *Sophia* at the first appears a woman of spirit, in opposing so vehemently the division of the Dukedom.
But

But she ill maintains this Character; when *Rollo* in her presence murders his Brother, threatens both her and her Daughter, she very tamely exhorts the Daughter to a vile compliance, says she

Rise Daughter, serve his will in what we may,
Least what he may not, he enforce the rather.
Is this all you command us?

She ought surely in another sort of tone to have resented this outrage, or before to have manifested a partiality for *Rollo*.

At his death History informs us she died of grief. 'Tis a wonder this Tragedy spares her; hers would have been a more decent and Poetical death then any of the rest. In this the History is the better Tragedy.

The Princess *Matilda* for the small part she bears, acquits her self bravely enough. Yet, methinks, *Aubrey* and she should have exchang'd some words; some glances have been cast, or otherways some approaches have
been

been begun. For here there scarce go three words to the bargain. In the last lines of the Play he comes to this Lady as abruptly as to the *Dukedom*, both drop into his mouth.

In Edith these waylings, clingings, and beseechings; these showers of tears and words.

---as you are a god above us,
Be as a god then full of saving
  pity,
Mercy, O Mercy Sir, for his sake
  Mercy,
That when your stout heart weeps,
  shall give you pity.
Here I must grow.

This sort of importunity is nothing so proper in this place, it might much better become *Comedy*, where Miss *La Fool* intercedes for little **Dog or Moncky**, in peril for some misdemeanor; something more of stomach and courage had suited her better. Tragedy requires not what is only Natural, but what is great in Nature, and such thoughts as quality and Court-education might inspire. She might indeed be surpriz'd, and at the first let the meer Natural woman escape

cape a little, but one or two so harsh and barbarous repulses should have rouz'd that Tragical spirit so vilely prostituted, and made her reflect on the other bloody scenes, so lately acted before her eyes, and caus'd her to despair before she had troubl'd us with her endless impertinencies.

Nor indeed comes short of her for tongue and wind, the old *Dutchess*, when in all reason one might expect that so violent grief and passions would choak them; they run chattering, as if the concern were no more then a *gossiping*: theirs are not of the old cut, *Curæ leves loquuntur ingentes stupent*.

Take her then resolv'd to kill this *Holofernes*, when she sets up for a *Heroine*, and will revenge the blood of the murder'd King *Otto*, of her Father, and the rest. When that scene presents her full of dire design and bloody purpose, we then indeed have her concise in word, and *Laconick* in the *repartee*. To the first Complement she answers.

Your

(45)

Your grace is full of game.
Wilt please you sit Sir.
Of what Sir.
Has a strange cunning tongue,
Why do you sigh Sir.
My anger melts, O I shall lose my justice.
His tongue will tempt a Saint.
He will fool me.

Is it likely that a Lady in her circumstances could be sensible what a pretty lisping way he had with him; or could listen to the soft things he spoke, or answer him so lightly? is not this more like some *Minx* in an Alley, then any Character for Tragedy? There are in Women comical frailties, and heroick frailties: and several considerations might have made her resolution stagger; but this of the *tempting tongue* is *Comedy* out of season.

I would also in this scene note this passage, says

Ham. Pray.
Roll. Pray.
Ham. Pray if thou canst pray, I will

will kill thy foul elfe.

Pray fuddenly.

This I think founds not fo well in Poetry, whatever it may do in Divinity. And now that I am upon the fhort Dialogues, let me cite one that went before.

Ham. *See Sir* Gisberts *head.*

Roll. *Good speed, was't with a Sword.*

Ham. *An Axe, my Lord.*

Roll. *An Axe,'twas vilely done.*

But leaving *Edith*, let us examine what was there in this *Latorch* to give him the afcendant over his Soveraign? Was it his Quality, his Valour, or fome Peftilent Wit, or what Fiddle had he to Charm this favage Mafter of his? (*a*) An Hiftorian (who was never taxt for a prodigal of his words) could not mention the *Dame* that led *Cataline* aftray, without annexing the Inventory of her Excellencies, as how well fhe Danc'd, how fhe handl'd the Lute, and how fhe fpoke Greek. Yet *Rollo* a Prince of as great importance to us, is led by the Nofe to do all the mifchiefs under

(a) *Saluft.*

the

the Sun; and no body knows who 'tis does manage him.

'Tis possible that a Prince may abandon himself to be rul'd by some busie creature of no consideration. The *Annals* of *Normandy* may mention such *Dukes*.

History may have known the like. But *Aristotle* cries shame. *Poetry* will allow of nothing so unbecoming, nor dares any Poet imagine that God Almighty would trust his Anointed with such a Guardian-Devil.

In the third *Act* enters *Hamond*, Captain of the Guard, and is a nimble Executioner; and who would guess this the Man ordain'd to kill the Dragon. But whether in Poetry this job more properly belong'd to *Edith*, or to this *Hamond*, may be a question.

In the first place 'tis resolv'd that to neither of them did it belong, but that (of the two) *Edith* might rather have kill'd *Rollo*, the following reasons may prove, *viz.*

1. To *Edith* the provocation was greater; a Father engaging our Piety more strongly then a Brother

2. *Ha-*

2. *Hamond* holding a place of truſt, had a ſtricter tye upon him: and *Edith* lying under no ſuch obligation; the fact in her would not have been ſubject to ſo many aggravations.

3. She, as a woman, might be preſum'd not ſo well to underſtand Allegiance, and to diſtinguiſh how far her Piety was to be reſtrain'd by it.

4. As in her ſex reaſon is ſaid to be more feeble, ſo the Paſſions are ſuppos'd to be the more violent and precipitate.

5. The puniſhment had been more ſignal and more grievous to the Tyrant, dying by the hand of a woman, and a woman to whom he was making love.

6. By a woman the fact would have been more ſurpriſing and extraordinary; and greater would have been the wonder, which a Poet always endeavours for, when it claſhes not with probability.

7. *Baldwin* was of better quality then *Allan*. For though the Maid might be content enough to be rob'd of her revenge; yet what would her
Fathers

Fathers Ghoſt ſay? And indeed what would the *Chancellor's* and *Otto's* Ghoſt ſay? was their blood dumb? or was not the cry of their blood to be heard? muſt they be murder'd and no harm enſue? only to the Manes of the Chancellors Man muſt this Monarch be ſacrific'd.

Allan *te hoc vulnere---* ſays *Hamond.*

Allan, my Brother *Allon* gives this ſtab.

Allon it ſeems is ſatisfi'd, whilſt his betters muſt be fain to appeal, and wait till *Doomſday.*

Hitherto the Plot and Caracters.

For the thoughts and good ſenſe, compare the ſpeech againſt dividing the Dukedom, with that in *Herodian* (from whence our Author takes it) on that ſame occaſion. Upon the diviſion it was agreed, the one Brother to have *Europe,* the other to have *Aſia;* which their Mother hearing, thus ſpoke;

The Sea and Land, my Sons, you have found how to divide; the Propontick, *you ſay, is a bound for either Continent, but how is it that*

E *you*

you will divide your Mother? how shall wretched I be cut in two and disposed on to each of you? first, therefore, first slay me, and each of you take his moiety with him, and bury it. So with the Sea and Land, I also shall be divided between you.

Says *Sophia*,
Divide me first, and tear me limb by limb,
And let them find as many several graves,
As there are Vilages in Normandy,
And 'tis less sin than so to weaken it.
To hear it mention'd, does already make me
Envy my dead Lord, & almost Blaspheme
Those powers which heard my prayers for fruitfulness.
And did not with my first birth close my womb.
To me alone my second blessing proves my first,
My first of misery, for if heaven
That gave me Rollo, there had stay'd his bounty,
And Otto, my dear Otto ne're had been,
Or

Or being had not been so worth my love;
The stream of my affection had run constant,
In one fair current all my hopes had been
Laid up in one, and fruitful Normandy
In this division had not lost her glories.
For as 'tis now, 'tis a fair Did-mond
Which being preserv'd entire, exceeds all value
But cut in pieces (though these pieces are
Set in fine gold by the best workmans cunning)
Parts with all estimation. So this Kingdom
As 'tis yet whole, the neighbouring Kings may covet
But cannot compass, which divided will
Become the spoil of every barbarous Foe
That will invade it.

The former speech seems to show a Woman of great spirit, labouring to contain her passion till she may utter her mind: But this latter seems to present a *well-breath'd* and *practis'd Scold*, who vents her passion and eases her mind by talking, and can weep and talk everlastingly.

In that of *Julia* we find but one *thought*, yet that follow'd close and press'd with all the vehemence that a strong passion might inspire; as may be easily apprehended by any who understand in *Virgil*,

It lachrymans, guttisque humectat grandibus ora.

She is not content to say, divide me, but to lay the Image before their eyes, and make the stronger impression. She will, *like the Sea and Land be divided*, be cut in two, be shar'd out to them, to each his moiety, &c.

But what a pother makes the old *Dutchess?* never *French* Author hash'd and kickshaw'd a little sense into so many words that signifie nothing

thing. She manages as if she were to hold forth by the glass: Had her passion after the first three words burst out at her eyes, had she wept and torn her hair, her *Rhetorick* had been more moving, and better understood, and she had acquitted her self Heroickly: But she falls off immediately, as if she had bolted out some rash thing at first, and was afraid of being ta'ne at her word; her tongue runs over her passion, and steals into matters that lean another way, and she talks as if she would talk the impression of her first words quite out of the hearers heads again. After the three first words she flies from the only thought that was proper, high enough, and proportionable to her passion: she is for being split in as many pieces as there are *Villages* in *Normandy*; which expression scatters the thought, breaks the resemblance and carries all remote from the occasion, and must in effect move but very indifferently. From thence she plunges into such impertinent and inconsistent wild *jargon* as is obvious to any man. That of the Diamond is a good thought in it self; but in this place comes very cold from her mouth, 'tis no more than if she had said, *Divide the Dukedom, divide me first, nay divide a Diamond,* &c. Naturally in a great passion none have leisure to ramble for comparisons, much less to compute the value of Diamonds whole or broken.

I question not the *Grammar*, nor how Poetical the stile is, I rest in the sense, nor had yet been so particular, but that I take all this Tragedy to be of the same *piece* for the writing, unless that scene of the *Astrologers*; and the Comical part, than which nothing can be more diverting.

Speeches of more matter I confess we have in the Play, and to *Latorch* we are oblig'd for them.

No friends, Sir, to your honour,
Friends to your fall, where is your
  understanding
The noble vessel that your full soul
  sail'd in,

Ribb'd

Ribb'd round with honours, where is that? 'tis ruin'd.
The tempest of a womans sighs has sunk it.
Friendship, take heed, Sir, is a smiling Harlot,
That when she kisses, kisses a soder'd friendship,
Piec'd out with Promises; O painted Ruine!

This *Latorch* alwaies *Cants* at this rate, and an extraordinary *Muse* attends him. We may, I think, conclude the success of this Play due chiefly to the Scenes for laughter, the merry jig under the Gallows, and where the Tragedy tumbles into the Kitchin among the Skoundrels that never saw buskin in their lives before. There the Pantler and Cook give it that relish which renders it one of the most followed entertainments in the Town.

A King and no King.

WEll fares it with Tragedy,
  (says an (a) *old stager)*
The title is no sooner known, but the
  Spectators see into the design,
And agree what they are to expect.
Name Oedipus, they know Laius was
  his Father,
Jocasta his Mother and all the gene-
  ration:
So there needs no more but hold up
  a finger,
The Curtain's drawn, and to't they go.
But ill is our condition,
We are fain to coin new words,
Explain what is past, present, and
  to come,
Yet never can be understood enough,
And without this ado whether Phidon
Or whether Chremes *enters, he is hist*
  off the Stage;
When as Teucer, Oedipus, *or* Peleus
Might come with authority.

(a) *Antiphanes apud Athen.*

Our Authors we see, never make use of the advantage which that *Comedian* envy'd so much in Tragedy. This Title gives no more light into the design, then had they call'd it *Hocus Pocus*; and indeed the name seems rather to promise a *Comedy*, and one might expect some sort of *Mammamouchy* King, or Cozen of *Duke Trinckelo's* for the Heroe of the Play.

The Plot is this:

The Queen of *Iberia*, *Arane*, had feign'd her self with child, and made use of *Gobrias's* Son to carry out the cheat. She afterwards proves truly with child, which came to be *Panthea*, durst not discover the first cheat, so that *Arbaces* (*Gobria's* Son) became actually King, is made really so by marrying *Panthea*.

The rest is all *Episode*.

In this Fable appears some proportion, shape, and (at the first sight) an *outside* fair enough, yet at the bottom we hardly find what is more choice, or more *exquisite* and more

per-

perfect than History. By the *turn* of the *Plot*, if we look on *Arane*, this Play might have been call'd *The Deceiver Deceiv'd*, if we look on *Arbaces*, the title might have been *The Fortunate Impostor*, *The lucky Sham*, or something of that kind; which shews a want of that *good sense* in it which Tragedy requires.

There might have been feigned some right to the Crown long contested between the two Families; (as ours of *York* and *Lancaster*) and bloody civil war ready to break out; when unexpectedly all grew husht and ended in a marriage; which (by a train long laid by *Gobrias*) took effect. This marriage should not have seem'd so advantageous to the false King, and his Father who brought it about; but by manifest reasons of *state* appear'd absolutely necessary for the good of the Kingdom, and above all things, desired and labour'd for by the relations of *Panthea*.

Whereas on the contrary, we find the Queen Mother attempting to poison

son this usurper, and see no reason to blame her endeavours.

What sets this *Fable* below History, are many *improbabilities*, and those of the worst sort; because they contribute nothing to the wonder. What more improbable, than that the Mother whose business it was to contrive the death of the Impostor, should never caution or inform her only Daughter, who had the right to the Crown, that *Arbaces* was none of her Brother, but her vassal, and so obstruct her love for him?

Nor is it likely that *Gobrias* should not have reserv'd some means to let his Son know the secret, that his Sons conduct and addresses to gain the Princess, might have been fashion'd accordingly.

The Characters are all *improbable* and *unproper* in the highest degree, besides that both these, their actions and all the *lines* of the Play run so wide from the *Plot*, that scarce ought could be imagin'd more contrary.

We blunder along without the least streak of light, till in the *last act* we
stumble

stumble on the *Plot*, lying all in a lump together; neither any tolerable direction to guide us thither; nor ought ingenious, just, or reasonable, that carries us from thence.

What find we in the Son of *Gobrias* that he must have the Princess and the Kingdom for her portion, save only that the Knave his Father will have it so?

Take his picture sent before him, and drawn by a friend. --*He is vainglorious, and humble, and angry, and patient, and merry, and dull, and joyful, and sorrowful, in extremity in an hour*--- Should we find underwritten *This is a King*, yet could not reason give way to our belief.

Kings of *Tragedy* are all Kings by the Poets *Election*, and if such as these must be elected, certainly no *Polish* Diet would ever suffer Poet to have a voice in choosing a King for them. Nor will it serve that *Arbaces* is not truly a King, for he is actually such, and intended for a true and rightful King before the Poet has done with him, what wants in Birth
the

the Poet should make up in his Merit, every one is to consent and wish him King, because the Poet designs him for one, 'tis (besides) observ'd that Usurpers generally take care to deserve by their conduct what is deny'd them by right.

We are to presume the greatest vertues, where we find the highest of rewards; and though it is not necessary that all *Heroes* should be Kings, yet undoubtedly all crown'd heads by *Poetical right* are *Heroes*. This Character is a flower, a prerogative, so certain, so inseparably annex'd to the *Crown*, as by no Poet, no *Parliament* of Poets, ever to be invaded.

Arbaces indeed is of a different mould, he no sooner comes on the Stage, but lays about him with his tongue at so nauseous a rate, Captain *Bessus* is all Modesty to him, to mend the matter his friend shaking an empty skull, says *'Tis pity that valour should be thus drunk*. Had he been content to brag only amongst his own Vassals, the fault might be more sufferable, but the King of *Armenia* is is his prisoner, he must bear the load of all; he must be swagger'd at; insulted over, and trampl'd on without any provocation. We have a *Scene* of his sufferings in each *Act* of the Play: *Bajazet* in the *Cage* was never so carried about, or felt half the barbarous indignities which are thrown on this unfortunate Prince by our monster of a King.

If the Poet would teach that victory makes a man insolent; he must at the same time make victory blush, and fly to the other side; as a just punishment for him that had abused her favours.

To the Queen-Mother his language is, *Plagues rot the adulterous Witch! thou worse than Woman dam'd---strumpet---whore! &c.* to his Father *Gobrias*;

Curses incurable, and all the evils
Man's body or his spirit can receive,
Be with thee.

To the Princess *Panthea* his supposed

posed Sister, after having cast her in Prison, and a thousand outrages very coarsly.

> Arb. *I have beheld thee with a lustful eye.*
> *My heart is set on wickedness, to act*
> *Such sins with thee, as I have been afraid*
> *To think of. If thou dar'st consent to this,*
> *(Which I beseech thee do not) thou mayst gain*
> *Thy liberty, and yield me a content:*
> *If not, thy dwelling must be dark and close.*

These speeches, drawing his Sword at the Queen-Mother, and the other outrages, make the sum of our *Heroes* vertues, and neither worse nor better find we throughout his character. *Arbaces* should have been consider'd in a double capacity; he should have been endu'd with all the greatness of mind, and *generosity* of a King a King, and also with the *modesty* of a Subject. The want of which, is a great aggravation of his fauls; for his carriage towards the Royal Captive, towards the Queen-Mother, towards the Princess, as he was a King, were insupportable, as *no King*, it was all abominable. History sometimes takes notice of a certain *instinct* which has strangely hinder'd many unnatural actions. A Poet, I am sure, ought always to have that *instinct*, or some good *genius* ready to serve his *Heroe* upon occasion, to prevent these unpleasant *shocking* indecencies, which otherwise might happen. This *instinct* should in *Arbaces* have begot a respect to his Father *Gobrias*, and have humbl'd him in the presence of such as were truly of the *Blood Royal*.

And far from *decorum* is it, that we find the King *drolling* and quibling with *Bessus* and his Buffoons, and worse, that they should presume to break their little jests upon him.

This too is *natural*, some will say. There are in nature many things which

which *Historians* are asham'd to mention, as below the dignity of an History: Shall we then suffer a *Tom Coriat* in *Poetry*? Shall we on the most important day of a King's Reign, and at Court be content with such entertainment as is not above a Cobler's shop? Might not a Poet as well describe to us how the King eats and drinks, or goes to *Stool*; for these actions are also *natural*: but observe the behaviour of *Arbaces*, after that he is found to be *no King*. Now he will make amends, and give satisfaction to all he had wrong'd. To the Gentlemen about him.

Arb. Why do you keep your hats off,
   Gentlemen?
Is it to me? I swear it must not
   be.
Nay, trust me, in good Faith it must
   not be.
I cannot now command you, but I
   pray you,
For the respect you bear me, when
   you took
Me for your King; each man clap

*On his hat
At my desire.*

And surely the Captive King cannot but be content, when told that

Arb. *He shall go so home, as never man went.*
Mardon. *Shall he go on's head?*
Arb. *He shall have Chariots easier than air,
That I will have invented; and ne'r think
He shall pay any ransom: And thy self
That art the Messenger shalt ride before him
On an Horse cut out of an intire Diamond,
That shall be made to go with golden Wheels.
I know not how, yet.*

For the Captive King's Mistress;

Arb. *She shall have some strange thing; we'l have the Kingdom
Sold utterly, and put into a toy,*
Which

Which she shall wear about her carelesly
Somewhere or other.

Now, that he is no King, nor has ought to give, he is for selling all without asking leave of the true Sovereign *Panthea*. To her his Compliment is,

Arb. *Grant me one request.*
Pant. *Alas, what can I grant you? what I can, I will.*
Arb. *That you will please to marry me.*
If I can prove it lawful.
Pant. *Is that all?*
More willingly than I would draw this air.

Should not rather the *Spirit* of *Majesty* have now rouz'd up in the Princess, and she have call'd to mind his late brutish insolence, and have call'd him impudent Slave, and discharg'd a frown that should have struck him dead, or commanded him to be *nail'd* to the floor as *false* coin,

and

and a *counterfeit* stamp of Majesty. And certainly his *character* could deserve no better fate. But for his comfort, this Princess was none of those. One might swear she had a knock in the Cradle; so soft she is at all points, and so silly. No *Linsey-woolsey* Shepherdess but must have more *soul* in her, and more sense of *decency* (not to say) honour. To this Vassal of hers, on her knees for half an hour together, she whines at this rate, *viz.*

 Pan. *I know I am unworthy, yet not ill*
 Arm'd, with which innocence I here will kneel
 Till I am one with earth; but I will gain
 Some words, and kind ones, from you.

Thus she continues, and by and by he *kisses her thrice*, then calls her *Witch*, *Poisoner*, *Traitor*, sends her to Prison; she thanks him with all her heart.

       Pan.

Nay, 'tis well the King is pleas'd with it.

At the next meeting she will needs be closer and closer to him; he cannot keep her off him, he tells her he would commit *incest* with her: She returns a drawling, yawning, yielding answer; and proceeds to tell him, that she wishes he were not her Brother, that she loves him so well, she can love no man else; she shall weep her eyes out: and farther.

Pan. *But is there nothing else That we may do, but only walk? methinks Brothers and Sisters lawfully may kiss.*

Had *Panthea* been some *Wastcoatteer* of the Village, that had been formerly *Complaisant* with him beyond discretion, more vile submissions she could not devise: But as she is lawful *Sovereign*, nothing could be invented more opposite to all *honesty*,

F 3 *honour,*

honour, and *decorum*. If we confider them as Brother and Sifter, 'tis horribly wicked. If we look on her as Sovereign, and him as her Subject, what can be more difhonourable? So that if *inftinct* guided their love, as lawful and warrantable; it may be anfwer'd, that the fame *inftinct* fhould have prevented that love, as infolent and prefumptuous in *Arbaces*, bafe and unbecoming in *Panthea*. For whether a Lady may better marry her Brother, or her Groom, is a queftion more eafily decided in Divinity, than in Poetry.

We are let to know that the Queen-Mother was for removing the Ufurper by poifon, and for bringing all into the right channel agen. This we might expect to be a Woman *couragious*, and truly *Tragical*: yet we find her the verieft *patient Griffel* that ever had lain by a Monarch's fide. She comes but thrice on the Stage; the firft time fhe is rebuk'd by *Gobrias*, with the fame language that the *Vicar* of *Newgate* might difpence to fome *finner* forlorn; then fhe is on her

her *mary-bones* to the Impoſtor without reluctancy. Laſtly, when provok'd with a drawn Sword, and words more cutting, the proudeſt rant ſhe could be rais'd to, was: --- *Fire conſume me if ever I was a Whore.*

If nothing elſe in the character of *Arbaces*, the drawing his *Sword* againſt a *Woman*, was enough in Poetry to damn him. After that *outrage*, he could make no pretenſions to ought that is good or honourable.

On this occaſion memorable is that paſſage in *Virgil*, where *Æneas* after having related, how the Town on fire about his ears, -- on the ſudden awak'd from his ſleep, -- flung headlong by rage and deſpair, -- forſaken by his reaſon, -- his friends ſlaughter'd about him, -- the King *Priam* murder'd before his face: -- when he ſpies the cauſe of all this, *Hellen*, skulking in a corner -- at the ſight of her.

Exarſere ignes animo, ſubit ira
  cadentem
Ulciſci patriam, & ſceleratas ſu-
  mere pœnas, &c.

All which, with what follows, comes to no more, than had he said; -- In that nick of time I even made a question within my self, whether I was not to take revenge on her; to that degree of madness had my troubles wrought me.

Talia jactabam, & furiata mente
   ferebar.

Now here, this revenge goes no farther than his thoughts; these thoughts---- *Æneas* himself condemns, and calls them madness; and is also sharply reprov'd for them by his *Guardian Angel,*

Nate, quis indomitas tantus furor
   excitat iras?
Quid furis?

No man but *Virgil* could ever pen any thing with that infinite care and caution as is this particular passage. One might think *Virgil* foresaw whatever could be objected; and provided against all scruples.

Yet

Yet of such a nice taſt were the *Criticks* in that *age* of *good ſenſe*; that *Varus* and *Tucca* ſtruck out all the 22 Verſes which contain this paſſage. Theſe were employ'd by *Auguſtus* to inſpect what (by the untimely death of *Virgil*) might have been left imperfect, and they durſt not ſuffer theſe 22 lines to paſs, though eſſential to the Poem; ſo tender they were, leſt their *Heroe* might lye under a ſuſpition of tránſgreſſing in any *punctilio* of that nature.

We need not make a controverſy whether *Virgil* or his *Criticks* be in the right: But if *Virgil* will not in a man allow the *thought* of ſtriking a Woman in any circumſtances, unleſs he condemns himſelf for that *thought*. And if his *Criticks* will not permit a *thought* of that kind with any *qualifications* whatſoever; then we may well conclude, that *Poetry* to be very *groſs*, where the *men* both think, and ſpeak, and act their *cruelties* againſt *Women*, without any ſhame or reſtraint.

But

But *Arbaces*, though mad, and flash'd upon by never so great a *hurrican* of provacations, was not to be allow'd to think of striking; because the Womans *quality* was above his, and made her sacred. Neither in this point is there a difference betwixt an *Epick* Poem and a *Tragedy*; when the conclusion of both is *prosperous*.

As here, *Æneas*, a King, of great merit, by the assistance of Heaven, and his friends, after much labour, marries *Lavinia*.

And *Arbaces*, no King, of no merit, without friends in Heaven, or on the Earth; without any trouble weds his King's only Daughter, and the Kingdom of *Iberia* is her portion.

I know with the Ancients, *Orestes* kill'd his Mother, *Hercules* his Wife and Children; *Agamemnon* his Daughter. But the first was an act of *Justice*; the second of *Frenzy*; the last of *Religion*. But these were all Tragedies unhappy in the *catastrophe*. And the business so well prepar'd; that every one might see, that these
Worthies

Worthies had rather have laid violent hands on themselves, had not their *will* and choice been over-rul'd. Every step they made, appear'd so contrary to their inclinations, as all the while shew'd them unhappy, and render'd them the most *deserving* of pitty in the World.

Another *Canker* in the heart of this *Tragedy*, is the incestuous love (for such it appears) between *Arbaces* and *Panthea*, I mean, the *conduct* of it. When any *design* on the *Stage* is in agitation, the Poet must take care that he engage the affections, take along the heart, and secure the good will of the Audience. If the *design* be wicked, as here the making approaches towards an *incestuous* enjoyment; the *Audience* will *naturally* loath and detest it, rather than favour or accompany it with their good wishes. 'Tis the sad effects and consequences of an ill *design* which the *Audience* love to have represented; 'tis then that the *penitence*, *remorse* and *despairs* move us: 'tis then that we grieve with the sorrowful,

ful, and weep with thofe that weep.

Therefore were the Ancients to make an *inceſtuous* love their fubject; they would *take* it in the *fall,* as it rowls down headlong to defperation and mifery.

Many in the *World* for their intereft may comply and help forward the *advances* towards an ill action; but on the *Stage* there is no kindred nor filthy lucre to biafs the *Audience,* or make them partial to the evil-doer. If the Poet obferve not thefe meafures, the *working up of a Scene,* is plainly the tormenting of nature, and holding our ears to the *Grindſtone.*

For an inceftuous love, famous amongft the Ancients, was the *tale* of *Macareus* and *Canace.* In the lift of thofe Tragedies wherein *Nero* delighted to be an *Actor, Suetonius* reckons *Canace parturiens.* The title may fatisfy us, that all the foft things, all the amours, the flowers and *fleurets* were over, e're the Offenders entred on the *Stage.*

In

In this last age a noble (*) *Italian* compos'd a Tragedy of *Canace* after the *model* of the Ancients; for the time of the *action*: he also chooses the day of *Canaces labour*. And then the pangs of child-bearing are the easiest that she suffers. For, to heighten the disgrace, this Poet feigns *Macareus* and *Canace* to be *Twins*, and this day to have been their birth-day, which the King, their Father, is about to solemnize with a Festival. Immediatly we find the two Offenders (under their apprehension of being discover'd) in the greatest confusion and despair imaginable. But that we might more justly pitty them, he informs us, that their crime proceeded not from any folly or miscarriage in themselves which they might have avoided ; but that a (†) *resistless power above*, and Cœlestial force had over-rul'd them : that indeed *Venus*

(*) *Speroni Sperone.*

(†) *Non malattia mortale,*
Mà fa celeste forza
Non propria elettione,
Mà un impeto fatal.——

had

had an old reck'ning with their *Father Æolus*, for persecuting her *Æneas*, and thus she discharg'd it with a *vengeance*.

By the rule of the Antients no colours, no sophistry or ribaldry's, were us'd to lessen a crime before it was committed: for then their Rhetorick could have no good effect, but must have *grated* on the hearers patience. But after the fact, when its punishment came heavy upon it, then all their art and invention was at work, to find out circumstances to extenuate the guilt, that the persons *guilty* might be capable of *pity*.

Arbaces in the dishonest love to his Sister, should have follow'd the example of that *Antiochus* in the History, who in love with his *Stepmother*, discover'd not his passion by any words or *gallantries*; but pin'd away, and gave himself over to dye; and had dy'd, if the dexterity of his Physitian had not by feeling his *Pulse* learnt the cause of his distemper.

The better to cleer this matter, I will trace the manners and conduct
of

of *Phedra* in *Euripides*, where we are told that *Hippolytus* having too rudely flighted the Altars of *Venus*, she is offended, and will have the whole Family feel the effects of her resentment. To bring this about, she strikes *Phedra* with a poison'd dart, and makes her in love with this *Hippolytus*, her Son in Law. *Phedra* conceals her love, strives to overcome it, not prevailing, resolves to (*a*) kill her self by fasting. And now for three days had she neither eat nor slept, when she first appears on the Stage. No wonder then if she talks very madly, she is in an hundred minds all at once, she tries all places and all postures, and is always uneasie in the present. *Now her dress is a pain to her, and now she will be carry'd to her Closet and shut up close, instantly agen, she calls to have her locks tied back, and nothing but the garb of an Amazon will please her, then she would sleep in some grott, and drink the waters from a mossie foun-*

(*a*) Ἀσιτεῖ δ' εἰς ἀπόστασιν βίου.

tain.

tain. Now she cries for the open air, for ranging the hills, for driving the woods, for whooping the dogs, for chasing the Stag, and brandishing a Javelin: and ah that the horses were ready to mount. Now she complains of her distraction, and blames some (b) *Divine power; and now her face is loaded with shame, confusion and tears. Hide me (she cries) ah hide me from the world, it pains her (she says) to return to her right senses.*

Here is a *Scene* of *Madness*, but not of *Bedlam*-madness; here is *Nature*, but not the *obscenities*, not the *blind-sides* of Nature, which are represented when *Arbaces* and *Panthea* go *loose* together, and whether of the two Madnesses is the more apt to move *pity*, need not certainly be a question.

Hitherto cannot the Governess, Confident, or *Nurse* of *Phedra*, understand where *Phedra* is pincht. She sifts, importunes and conjures her, yet

(b) Ἐμάνην ἐποίν δαίμονος ἄτη.

after

after all is no wiser till accidentally amongst other arguments whereby she would perswade *Phedra* to live, *Live*, says she, *otherwise you betray your Children to be Lorded over by that other womans Bastard, this* Amazon's *Son, I mean* Hippolytus, *woes me*, says *Phedra*, *you have undone me! name him no more.* The Nurse proceeds to torture her with questions, and *Phedra* returns as many perplexed answers, till at the last says *Phedra*,

Phed. *What is it that men call to be in love?*
Nurse. *It is of all things the sweetest, and also the most bitter.*
Phed. *I have sufficiently experienc'd both.*
Nurse. *What says my Child, do you love any Man?*
Phed. *Who is that same, that of the* Amazon?
Nurse. *Say you* Hippolytus?
Phed. *This from your self you hear; but not from me.*

Alas!

Alas! undone! intolerable, cries the Nurse, and she will not live one moment longer. And concludes that all, (even modest women too against their will) would be naught, and that Love is the veryest god almighty; there is not the fellow of him in all the heavenly gang

I have only cited the conclusion of this *Scene*, to note the utmost *advances* of *Phedra* towards a confession, the only crime of which she was guilty; and to show that this Nurse (so long kept in ignorance) was no fool, but subtle and nimble enough to catch and run away with the least *hint* that could be offer'd.

In the former Scene all the conflict was between love and modesty; this presents *love* and an active *friendship* join'd, both at once labouring to subdue this *modesty*, so far only as to extort a confession. The *Nurse* with wrung hands lies at *Phedra's* feet, embraces her knees, begs her to live, for her Childrens sake to live, and tell her pain. *Phedra* strives, would be from the Nurses hands, complains of the

the violence, promises to tell, yet raves and rambles, speaks short and ambiguous, all is darkness; whilest every where tenderness, passion and modesty reign, and appear to admiration.

This *Scene* having wrought off the *Remains* of *Phedra's* frenzy, in the next she seems more calm, her mind more at ease, and now will move *pity* from a new *Topick*, for now this unfortunate Lady is found to be a woman of *great sense* and understanding. *She reasons (to the Chorus) and wonders how humane life becomes so corrupt, for certainly (says she) it cannot be natural to do amiss, when we understand what is right. Yet thus it happens, we have before our eyes, and know what is good, but we practise otherwise. Some out of sloath, and others preferring a kind of pleasure before honesty; there be many pleasures of life, as conversation, ease a sweet evil, and modesty. Now there are two sorts of pleasure, one good; the other the bane of Families: but would this appear always in its true colours, 'twould no longer be counted pleasure. These things when I consider'd, I thought no* Philter *could ever seduce me to act against my knowledge.*

But to open my mind to you, after love had wounded me, I cast with my self how I might bear my illness the most decently, and from that time made it my care to hide my distemper and keep it to my self. Secondly, I resolv'd to get my right senses agen, and with chastity to overcome my frenzy. In the third place, if the attempt to cure my distemper prov'd vain, I then thought my best course would be to dye.

For I know the disease to be infamous, and especially in me a woman, odious to all people.

Then she curses those *who first polluted the Marriage-bed.* And *hates the baggages that can talk so smoothly, and yet will do naughty things in a corner.* (a) *Blessed Lady*, says she,

---

(a) Πῶς ποτ' ὦ δέσποινα πότνια κύπρι.

how

how can they look their husbands in the face? how can they but tremble at their (b) *confederate darkness? and be afraid that the very* (c) *walls and doors should open and cry whore at 'um.*

She concludes, *Therefore dear friends, this same shall kill me, that I may never be taken to disgrace my Husband, and the Children I have brought forth.*

The *Nurse* perceiving her Mistress thus resolute, sets her tongue a running to this purpose.

Lady (quoth she) I was lately in a twittering fear for you,
But now I confess my self hen-hearted.
It has been said, that second thoughts are the wisest.
And now (believe me) there is nothing singular,

(b) ——τὸν συνεργάτην.

(c) ——τέρεμνα τ᾽ οἴκων.

G 3   *Nothing*

Nothing unreasonable in your case.
The truth is, the goddess is terrible angry at you.
Well, you love? that's no marvel.
And you would kill your self for love.
That wou'd be a pleasant pranck, if all that are,
And that are to be in love must presently take that course.
There is no striving,
No dodging with love, when it comes in earnest.
'Tis easie to those that are yielding.
But if you will be goodly, and think high of your self,
If you will resist and be stubborn,
Why, then there's no whoo with it,
It shakes and breaks, and thunders you to Atoms immediately.
Love is King of the air,
Whizz goes his power through the blew seas,

And

And we are all of us his off-
spring.
They who have read the Chroni-
cles,
Or are skill'd in antient Bal-
lades,
Can tell us stories of Jupiter, Seme-
le, Cephalus.
Of such love, and such wild lo-
vers as you wou'd think strange
at.
Yet these Lovers (many of them)
were * *prefer'd in heaven,*
And now are waiting at gods ell-
bow.
The gods melted with their suffer-
ings, cou'd not be angry.
And now you will be in a fit.
You cannot be content with the same
Laws,
With the same Nature, with flesh
and blood, like other folks.
You should have been hatch'd in Ju-
piter's *brain,*

* ἀλλ' ὅμως ἐν ὐρανῶ

ναίεσι, κ̓ φέυγεσιν ἐκποδῶν θεός.

G 4   *And*

And so been fram'd some blessed Angel.
How many men who are right in their senses,
See their bed tumbl'd, yet walk on,
And lets it trouble their heads no farther.
'Tis nine points of wisdom to keep that secret,
Which would be no credit, when divulg'd.
Perfection is an aiery notion, never to be found in practice.
Then surely they are well hop't up,
Who set themselves to live (a) *exactly.*
As this world goes, if our good deeds out-tell the bad,
We shall make an handsome reck'ning.
Then, dear Child, be no longer in an ill mind,
For the goddess has an heavy pique against you.
And trust not that she will be check-mated by you.

(a) ἀκριβώσαι.

Nor

*Nor think you to be higher than
the highest of all:
For such, in effect, is your last reso-
lution.
And, to tell you plainly, 'tis an af-
front to 'em.
Then pluck up a good heart,
And love on; since* (b) **God will
have it so.**
*You have a wound, cure your wound.
There are Spells, and Charms, and
(c) healing words,
Some remedy shall be found out for
you.
And truly, if we Women cannot
advise you,
The wit of man will come too late.*

The *Nurse* here delivers all the *good sense* that could be proper for the occasion, as may be discern'd, notwithstanding the ill dress, in which I have disguis'd it. A less considering Poet would have displaid all this *dialogue-wise*, and made it a Scene of

(b) ——Θεὸς ἐβουλήθη τάδε.

(c) ——λόγοι θελκτήριοι.

mighty

mighty sputter. But *Euripides* would not suffer his *Phedra* so far to countenance or listen to these lewd reasons, as once to think they deserv'd any particular answer. To dispute in a matter of this kind, would have been the next door to the being convinc'd; and to contend, was to put her self in the way of being overcome. She therefore at once makes this return.

>Ph. *'Tis thus that Towns and Kingdoms are destroy'd,*
>*By a fair tongue and flattering speech decoy'd:*
>*We should not file our words to please the ear;*
>*But strike the mind, and kindle glory there.*

To make short, *the Nurse tells her that wise* sentences *will not do the business: that, for her part, she would not be the minister of any ones pleasure: but in this extremity, where life is at stake, she might without blame, for a violent disease, provide an extraordinary Cure.* Phe-

Phedra calls these *horrible, filthy speeches;* and commands *her to* (*) *lock up her mouth.*

The Nurse urges *that her words, if they are not clean, they are wholsome; and the preservation of life was of more importance than any proud name she would boast on in her death.*

But she (finding that this sort of discourse did the more exasperate and provoke her Mistress) recants. *But (says she) now that it comes in my mind, I have at home* (†) *healing Philters that will work your Cure without touching upon your modesty.*

Phedra is in fear, makes scruples, asks questions; which the Nurse evades, and tells her, *she wanted not to be instructed, but to be assisted.*

In the next *Scene Phedra* is on the Stage, and over-hears the Nurse within, exchanging some words with *Hippolytus:* whereupon she cries out

(*) ἐχὶ συγκλείσυς ϛόμα

(†) ἔϛιν κατ᾽ οἴκυς φίλτρα μοι θελκτήρια.

says,

says, she is betraid, curses the Nurse, and resolves to kill her self. And now the apprehensions that *Hippolytus* would accuse her to his Father, made her write a Letter, laying all the blame on *Hippolytus*, as the best expedient (that amidst her distractions, she could on the sudden devise) to *secure* her *honour*, and to prevent the *disgrace* of her *Family*, and of her *Children*: and with this Letter in her hand, she hangs her self.

Had some Author of the last age given us the character of *Phedra*, they (to thicken the *Plot*) would have brought her in burning of Churches, poisoning her Parents, prostituting her self to the Grooms, folliciting her Son face to face, with all the importunity and impudence they could imagin; and never have left dawbing so long as there might remain the least cranny for either *pitty* or *probability*. They would never have left her, till she had swell'd to such a *Toad*, as nothing but an *audience* of *brass* could fit the sight of her.

But (for our credit) *Seneca*, before us,

us, in this *blind* way of *designing* made no inconsiderable progress. We find his *Phedra* at the first dash justifying her *incestuous* love: and her Nurse is the Woman of *sentences*; who labours with all the wholsome advise, the sense and nonsense she could scrape together, to *maul* this monstrous lust that rag'd in her Nursling, *Phedra*. And whilst she goes on without any signs of success, *Phedra* surprises her, (on the sudden) resolving to *dye* with a good name. Whereupon the Nurse bids her be patient, and promises to try what she can do with the young man.

Without more words, the next *Scene* presents us *Phedra*, (as if the late resolution had never been made) all upon the *gallantry*, she is tricking her self up in *Masquerade*; and thus she hopes to win the Salvage *Hippolytus*, and the Nurse and she make their supplications to the Goddess of *Chastity* to help on their design. And now it is that the Nurse attacks him: but how? she expounds to him at large, that a *City-life* and *Women* are

a coma comfortable *importance*; he anſwers in another *harangue*, that nothing is like to the *ranging* in the Countrey: and truly (for *Women*) he hates them all mortally. During this conference, *Phedra* reels in amongſt them, falls in a ſwoun; and well is it for her that ſhe is taken up in the arms of her beloved Son: therefore ſhe takes heart, and puts it to him couragiouſly. But words proving vain, ſhe will needs (a) *raviſh* the poor ſtripling. Hereupon, to cut her neck off, he draws out the brown Faulcheon, (b) on which ſhe laying her ſweaty palms, he cries foh! flings it from him, and runs away. And now the Nurſe puts in her word, and ſays, *marry*, 'tis the beſt way to be before-hand with him, and to cry Whore firſt. Accordingly they fly to *Theſeus*, *Phedra* tells him that *Hippolytus* not only purpoſed, but had (c) effected his filthy pur-

(a) *Etiam in amplexus ruit?*
Stringatur enſis.

(b) *Contactus enſis deſerat caſtum latus.*

(c) *Vim tamen corpus tulit.*

poſe

pose upon her body, do she what she could: and *ecce signum* shews the Sword to witness for her truth. Hereupon *Theseus* dispatches his Son *Hippolytus* into another World. And now (with a canker to her) comes *Phedra*, confesses the truth indeed, and kills her self.

Now in this *Phedra* of *Seneca*, what one occasion of *pitty* have we? what ground for *terror*? and, above all, what *manners* have we? ask the generality of Women if they are mov'd and concern'd, if their hearts and good will go along and attend the thoughts and motions of this *Phedra*? will they not answer that they know no such Woman, that she is no way a kin to them, nor has any resemblance with their nature? She must be some brat of a *Succubus*, or an evil *Spirit*, (say they) that personates a Woman; or some *Devil* in a *Machine*, that comes to render the Sex odious. Nor can they allow her more compassion than to a Bitch, or *Polecat*, and what has no relation to human shape.

Nor

Nor can this be a cause of *terror:* for few Women would be apt to fancy that they could (in any circumstances) be so wicked as this *Phedra.* Each will say, were it my fate, or should I be curst to love where I ought not, I would certainly conceal my love, and strive with it, my thoughts, words, and actions, and all, my condition might be every way the same, or very like to that of *Phedra* in *Euripides.* But I could never speak or act at this impudent abominable rate, could never be transform'd to such a monster as this *Phedra* of *Seneca.* And since my conduct would not be the same, my case can never be the same; and consequently this *example* cannot move or concern, or have any operation to stir either *pitty* or *terror* in me.

I have been the more large on this matter, because it may serve as a certain and general *test*, whereby may be discover'd what is *naturally* apt to move *pitty* or *terror*. And this is founded on a Philosophy never contraverted, but alike current at *Malmsbury* as at *Athens.* Eve-

Every one have noted *Seneca* for his *unnatural* way of writing. Yet, besides what is already observ'd in his *characters*, I cannot leave him, without reminding you, that though he takes all his *thoughts* from *Sophocles* and *Euripides*, yet he rarely affords us any of their *good sense*. He crumbles every *thought* into all the little *points* that ever he can strain it to; and all these *points* (for, or against him, it matters not) must one way or other be apply'd.

Whensoever he finds a *Diamond*, he forces, and breaks it into an hunder'd pieces; never letting it rest so long as any of it will *sparkle*. I desire your patience but for one instance of this kind.

In the *Scene* where the *Nurse* presses to know what it is that pains her Mistress; amongst her other ravings, says *Phedra* in *Euripides*.

(a) *What sort of love lov'dst thou, ah wretched Mother?*

(a) ὦ τλῆμον, οἷον μῆτες ἠράσθης ἔρων

H *And*

And thou, unhappy Sister, Wife of Bacchus?
The third unhappy, I.

The Poet made *Phedra* say this, not only, as a proper and *natural* reflection, that these extravagant loves run in the blood; but as a *hint* of her disease, and withal so *qualifi'd*, as might also shew her *modesty*: for she puts less in the *conclusion* than was in the *premisses*. She *concludes* to the *unhappiness* only, and does not (as she might) say.

And now the third unhappy Lover, I.

We find *Seneca* baiting this *thought* six several times in one *Scene*, and we have at least, 40 lines in the **Tragedy** all meer *descant* upon it.

Ph. *Fatale* (a) *miseræ matris agnosco malum,*
Peccare noster novit in sylvis amor, &c.

Phed.

Ph. *Aut quis juvare.* (b) *dædalus flammas queat, &c.*

Nat. ----- (c) *Quid domum infamem gravas*
Superasq; matrem?

Nat. (e) *Memorq; matris metue concubitus novos.*

Nu. *Cur monstra cessant? aula cur fratris vacat?*
Prodigia toties orbis insueta audiet,
Natura toties legibus cedat suis,
Quoties *Amabit* Cressa?

Nu. *Patris memento:* Ph. (d) *Meminimus matris simul.*

Nu. *Adoritq; genitor.* Ph. *Mitis*
(f) Ariadnæ *pater.*

Hipp. *O majus ausa matre monstrifera malum,*
Genetrice peior! illa se tantum stupro
Contaminavit, & tamen tacitum diu
Crimen biformi partus exhibuit nota;
Scelusq; matris arguit vultu truci
Ambiguus infans; ille te venter tulit.

Ph. ———————— *Aut quis* Cressius
(c) *Dædalea vasto Claustra mugitu replens*
Taurus biformis, ore Cornigero ferox
Divulsit ?

The *thought* in *Euripides* was good and just enough; but here we have it hall'd, and pull'd, and tost, and tumbl'd about, in all postures and figures, and in all colours but the right. Observe but how a *a propos* the *Heroine* first starts it. *No wonder* (says she) *if my love goes to the* (a) *wood, seeing my Mother was gallanted by a Bull*; this brings her the ready way to (b) *Dædalus* and the *labyrinth*, where both she and the Poet are lost together. One might think, it would well enough serve from the Nurses mouth for an (c) use of reproof: till shortly after we find it a (d) *turn-coat*, and muster'd up by *Phedra* in the way of an excuse. The rest are all wide from sense and sobriety, as (e) *the huge bellowings that fill'd the Dædalian Cloysters.*

This

This may suffice for *Seneca*, and *Phedra*, with whom I had not so long digress'd, but that I had *Panthea* in mine eye all the while. Nor should I have judg'd *Panthea* worth all this ado, but that she has many proper Cousins on the Stage. And these vile characters have so long prosper'd, that they bear high, and are fairly on to pass for excellencies.

But I grow weary of this Tragedy: In the former I took *Latorch* by his mouth, and ranting air for a copy of *Cassius* in *Shakespear*: and that you may see *Arbaces* here, is not without his *Cassian* strokes.

Thus *Cassius* in *Shakespear*.

Cass. ---- Brutus *and* Cæsar! *what should there be in that* Cæsar! *Why should that name be sounded more than yours? Write them together, yours is as fair a name: Sound them; it doth become the mouth as well:*

Weigh them, it is as heavy; conjure with them, man:
Brutus *will start a Spirit as well as* Cæsar.
Now, in the name of all the Gods at once,
Upon what meat doth this our Cæsar *feed,*
That he is grown so great? ----

Thus *Arbaces.*

Arb. *I have liv'd*
To conquer men, and now am overthrown
Only by words, Brother and Sister; where
Have those words dwelling? I will find 'em out,
And utterly destroy 'em: but they are
Not to be grasp'd: let 'em be men or beasts,
I will cut 'em from the earth; or Towns,
And I will raze 'em, and then blow 'em up:

Let

*Let 'em be Seas, and I will drink
'em off,
And yet have unquench'd fire within my breast :
Let 'em be any thing but meerly
voice.*

Would not these raptures have put Sir *Will. Petty* in mind of the *Irish* Inscription?

FOR FIERCENESS AND
FOR FURIOUSNESS,--

MEN CALL ME THE QUEENS
MORTER-PIECE.

The business of the *Maids Tragedy* is this;

AMintor *contracted to* Aspatia *(*Callianax's *Daughter) by the* King's *command, marries* Evadne, *Sister to* Melanthius; *and expects to lye with her; but the Bride (mincing nothing) flatly tells him that he is but taken for a Cloak; that She, indeed, is a Bedfellow only for the* King. *The good man is perswaded to dissemble all, till his friend* Melanthius *extorts from him the secret: and thereupon hectors his Sister* Evadne *into repentance, and makes her promise to murder the* King. *Which she effects: in the mean time, by vexing* Callianax, Melanthius *prevails with him to deliver up the Fort, (wherein consisted the strength of the Kingdom,) and so provides for his own security.* Lysimachus, *Brother*

(105)

ther to the murder'd King, succeeds on the Throne, and pardons all. Evadne *would now go to bed with her Husband, he refuses, she kills her self.* Aspatia *in mans habit kicks her Sweetheart* Amintor, *duels him, and is kill'd: and now* Amintor *kills himself to follow her: at which sight, his friend* Melanthius *would also take the same course, but is prevented.*

Here we find *Amintor* false to his Mistress; and this fault is the source of all the revolutions in this Tragedy.

Amintor therefore should have named the Tragedy, and some additional title should have hinted the Poet's design.

But seeing the *Maid* comes in at the latter end, only, to be kill'd for company; and seeing the King is the person of greatest importance, is the greatest loser and concern'd in the action of the Play more than enough. And seeing that the new King *Lysimachus* in the close of the Tragedy makes this sober conclusion, says he;

May

May this a fair example be to me,
To rule with temper: for on lustful Kings
Unlookt-for sudden deaths from heaven are sent.
But curst is he that is their instrument.

From these considerations we might gather that the Poets intent was to show the dismal consequences of *fornication*. And if so, then the Title of the Tragedy should have related to the King.

Whil'st thus we are uncertain what ought to be the *title* we may suspect that the *Action* of the Tragedy is *double*, where there seem two centers, neither can be right; and the lines leading towards them must all be false and confus'd; the *preparation* I mean, and conduct must be all at random, since not directed to any one certain end.

But what ever the Poet design'd; nothing in *History* was ever so *unnatural,*

tural, nothing in *Nature* was ever so *improbable*, as we find the whole conduct of this Tragedy, so far are we from any thing accurate, and Philosophical as Poetry requires.

This will appear as we examin the particular actions and Characters apart.

Our Poet here gives to the great Comical *Booby Callianax*, the honour of a long name with a King at th'end on't, yet lets the King himself go without. But since he must be nameless we may treat him with the greater freedom, and to tell my mind, certainly God never made a King with so little wit, nor the devil with so little grace, as is this King *Anonymus*.

A King of History might marry his Concubine to another man for a Maid; might hinder that man from the enjoyment. But would not then turn them into the bed-chamber to be all night together; nor would come in the morning to interrogate and question him, and torture the soul of him, as we find in this Tragedy,

nor

nor would impose it on a husband thus affronted, whom he calls *honest* and *valiant*, to be the pimp to his bride. To have taken *Amintors* head off had been clemency in comparison of these outrages without any cause or colour. And how wise the King was in all this, may be judg'd from his own mouth, finding the husband contented and all quiet, the King (jealous that *Evadne* had not observ'd covenants) thus taxes her.

> *Do not I know the uncontrolled thoughts*
> *That youth brings with him, when his blood is high*
> *With expectation and desire of that*
> *He long had waited for? is not his spirit*
> *Though he be temperate of a valiant strain,*
> *As this our age has known? what could he do,*
> *If such a sudden speech had met his blood,*
>   *But*

But ruine thee for ever? if he had not kill'd thee,
He could not bear it thus; he is as we.
Or any other wronged man.

As if she had said, you have *Evadne*, you have broken Articles with me; it cannot be otherwise; for had you kept them, flesh and blood could not endure the affront, and he is such a man as would have cut us all to pieces in revenge. The danger being so cleer and certain, and a thousand safe courses before his nose, why should he stumble on this? never was a King of History so errant a fool and madman.

In framing a Character for Tragedy, a Poet is not to leave his reason, and blindly abandon himself to follow fancy; for then his fancy might be monstrous, might be singular and please no body's *maggot* but his own, but reason is to be his guide, reason is common to all people, and can never carry him from what is Natural.

Many are apt to mistake *use* for *nature,*

nature, but a Poet is not to be an Historiographer, but a Philosopher, he is not to take *Nature* at the *second hand*, soyl'd and deform'd as it passes in the customes of the unthinking vulgar.

The (a) *Phedra* in *Euripides* told us truly that it is *not Natural to do evil when we know good*. Therefore vice can never please unless it be painted and dress'd up in the colours and disguise of vertue, and should any man knowingly and with open eyes prefer what is evil, he must be reckon'd the (b) greatest of Monsters, and in no wise be lookt on as any image of what is Natural, or what is suitable with humane kind.

What is there of the *Heroe*, of Man, or of Nature in these Kings of our Poets framing? And for *Evadners*

(a) κοίμοι δοκοῦσιν ἓ κατὰ γνώμης φύσιν πράσσειν κάκιον.

(b) ---*majus est monstro nefas*
Nam monstra fato, moribus scelera imputes.

Sen.

part, did Hell ever give reception to such a Monster? or *Cerberus* ever wag his tayl at an impudence so *sa-cred*?

On the Wedding night the Bride-room is cajol'd by her in no better :rms than.

Evad. A mayden-head, Amintor, *at my years?*
Alas, Amintor, *thinkest thou I forbear*
To sleep with thee. because I have put on
A Mayden strictness; look upon these cheeks
And thou shalt find the hot and rising blood
Unapt for such a vow; no, in this heart
There dwells as much desire, and as much will
To put that wish't all in practice, as ever yet
Was known to woman, and they have been shown
Both; but it was the folly of thy youth,

To

To think this beauty (to what land so e're
It shall be call'd) shall stoop to any second.
I do enjoy the best, and in that height
Have sworn to stand or dye.
Soon after she tells him.
Alas I must have one
To Father Children, and to bear the name
Of husband to me, that my sin may be
More honourable.

Hitherto she is bashful, after this the *Scene* is to be *wrought* up, and the next Scene presents her impudence *triumphant*; but I shall trace her duty towards her husband no farther.

Had *Evadne* been the injur'd bodies sister, and had marry'd *Amintor* out of revenge, or had their been any foundation from circumstances for this sort of carriage, the Character then might have been contriv'd plausible enough; but both the Kings be-

behaviour and hers, uncircumstanc'd as we have them, are every way so harsh and against Nature, that every thing said by them strikes like a dagger to the souls of any reasonable *audience*.

Whatever persons enter upon the Stage the Poetry would be gross enough if the audience could not by the *manners* distinguish in what Country the *Scene* lay; whether in *England, Italy*, or *Turky*: more gross would it be if the manners would not discover which were men and which the women.

Now Nature knows nothing in the *manners* which so properly and particularly distinguishes woman as doth her modesty, consonant therefore to our principles and Poetical, is what some writers of Natural History have reported; that women when drowned swim with their faces downwards, though men on the contrary.

Tragedy cannot represent a woman without modesty as natural and essential to her.

If a woman has got any accidental historical impudence, if documented in the School of *Nanna* or *Heloiſa*, ſhe is furniſh'd with ſome ſtock of acquired impudence, ſhe is no longer to ſtalk in Tragedy on her high ſhoes; but muſt rub off and pack down with the Carriers into the *Provence* of Comedy, there to be kickt about and expos'd to laughter.

There are degrees of modeſty. *Evadne* and every perſon feign'd ought to be repreſented with more modeſty then *Phedra* or *Semiramis*, becauſe the Hiſtory makes it credible that theſe had leſs of modeſty then Naturally is inherent to the Sex, yet ought theſe alſo to ſhow more of modeſty then is ordinarily ſeen in men, that the Characters might ſtill be diſtinguiſh'd.

But (of all) the Kings murder is attended with thoſe circumſtances, with ſuch a knot of abſurdity and injuſtice, that I well know not where to begin to unravel it.

This King indeed is born a Monſter, a Monſter of great hopes, and
what

what might we not have expected from him? yet certainly the Poet cuts him off, e're ripe for punishment.

And by such unproper means, that to remove one guilty person he makes an hundred; and commits the *deadly* sins to punish a *venial* one.

If *Amintors* falshood and its fatal consequences are to be noted, what occasion have we for a King in this Tragedy? cannot *Corydon* deceive his *Amaorillis* (for such is *Aspatia*) but the King must know of it, the King must be murder'd for't?

To vex this false man, a Groom might have done the job, and have been the Poets Cuckold-maker to all intents and purposes every jot as well.

If it be said that the King was accessary to the falshood, I question whether in Poetry a King can be an accessary to a crime, if the King commanded *Amintor*; *Amintor* should have begg'd the Kings pardon; should have suffer'd all the racks and tortures a Tyrant could inflict; and from *Perillus*'s Bull should have still bellowed out that eternal truth, that his *Promise was to be kept*, that he is true to *Aspatia*, that he dies for his Mistress, then would his memory have been precious and sweet to after-ages; and the Midsummer-Maydens would have *offer'd* their Garlands all at his grave.

And thus the King might kill *Amintor*, but *Amintor* could not pretend that the King or Fortune had made him false.

--- nec nisi miserum fortuna Sinonem
Finxit, vanum etiam mendacemque improba finget.

Therefore, I say, the King was not to blame; or however not so far, as in any wise to render his life obnoxious.

But if the Poet intended to make an example of this King, and that the King right or wrong must be kill'd. *Amintor* only felt the highest provocations,

cations, and he alone should have been drawn out for the wicked instrument, for *Melantius* had no reason to be angry at any but at his Sister *Evadne*; nor could she have any pretence to exercise her hands, unless it were against her self.

If I mistake not, in Poetry no woman is to kill a man, except her quality gives her the advantage above him, nor is a Servant to kill the Master, nor a Private Man, much less a Subject to kill a King, nor on the contrary.

Poetical decency will not suffer death to be dealt to each other by such persons, whom the Laws of Duel allow not to enter the lists together.

There may be circumstances that alter the case, as when there is a sufficient ground of partiality in an *Audience*, either upon the account of *Religion* (as *Rinaldo*, or *Riccardo* in *Tasso* might kill *Soliman*, or any other *Turkish* King or great *Sultan*) or else in favour of our *Country* for then a private *English Heroe* might overcome

come a King of some Rival Nation.

But grant that *Evadne* lies under none of all these impediments; suppose her duly qualifi'd, and let the King wave his priviledges. Is there in History any president of a *Magdalen* sinner, that meerly from a fit of repentance fell foul on her *Gallant* at this horn'd rate. Indeed, amongst 'em, they call him *lustful Thief, Devil-King, shameless Villain, &c.* the *Athenian* Servants were better bred.

(*a*) ὦ μῶρος, εἰ χρὴ δεσπότας εἰπεῖν τόδε.

Ah fool; if we may term our Masters so.

ὄλοιτο μὲν μή· μὴ δεσπότης γὰρ ἐστ' ἐμός.

Death take him! no, he is my Master.

But I say, what reason is there for all this outcry? What can she lay to the King's charge?

(*a*) *Euripides.*

Thou

*Thou kept'st me brave at Court,
and Whor'd me;
Thou marri'd me to a young noble
 Gentleman,
And whor'd me still.*

The *noble Gentleman* indeed is wrong'd: but, good Madam, what reason is there for you to complain? did any force or philter overcome you? was not you as forward? did not you freely and heartily consent? do not we remember your *hot rising blood.*

*--- Your much desire, and as much
 will
To put that wish'd act in practise,
 as ever yet
Was known to Woman?*

Has the King cast you off? or broken articles? no: but you repent? then repent at home; you may make bold with your own body, and there let fly your rage and violence. For to kill your Lover, is no effect or operation of repentance, nor has any ground in nature or reason : 'tis worse than brutish.

But indeed most of our Murderers hitherto have been no better; they are the Poets Ban-dogs let loose to worry those the Poet had mark'd out for slaughter; and never shew more reason or consideration : and consequently can in no wise occasion either pitty or terror to cause that delight expected from Tragedy.

In *Epick Poetry* enemies are kill'd; and *Mezentius* must be a wicked Tyrant; the better to set off Æneas's piety. In Tragedy, all the clashing is amongst friends, no *panegyrick* is design'd, nor ought intended but pitty and terror : and consequently no shadow of sense can be pretended for bringing any wicked persons on the Stage. And yet in that *Mezentius* of *Virgil*, we find more vertue than in all the characters I have yet examind; and greater occasion for pitty. We forget all his cruelties, when we see that trouble and infinite passion for his Son *Lausus*, (who was
slain

slain in his defence, and whom he would not survive,) which is so admirably exprest.

> ------ *Æstuat ingens*
> *Imo in corde pudor, mistoq; insania luctu,*
> *Et furiis agitatus amor, & conscia virtus, &c.*

Which lines, *Tasso* (who translates the whole passage under the names of *Solimano* and *Amiralto* into his *Gerusalemme*) thus renders in more words, but not with more advantage.

> *Ferue in mezzo del cor lo sdegno e l'onta,*
> *E co'l lutto la rabbia e mista insieme,*
> *E da le furie l'agitato amore,*
> *E noto a se medesmo l'empio valore.*

But to return, what yet makes this fact of *Evadne* more unlikely, is, that she should be hector'd into a repentance so pernicious, by her Brother

ther *Melantius*: who is said to be *noble* and *brave*; but from his own mouth we may judg him a *Heroe*, like those we met with formerly; all his words are brags; no *Dangerfield*, nor Captain *Thundergun* could sit neer him. And for his manners, after one King was murder'd by his contrivance, he stands on his guard, and takes up the next King thus roundly.

>Mel. *The short is this,*
>*'Tis no ambition to lift up my self,*
>*Urges me thus: I do desire again*
>*To be a Subject, so I may be freed;*
>*If not, I know my strength, and will unbuild*
>*This goodly Town; be speedy and be wise*
>*In a reply.*

And now this new King, Brother to the former, as *heroickly* throws him a *blank*, and bids him make his own

own terms. His words are thefe:

Lif. Melanthius, *write in that thy choice;*
My Seal is at it.

And more to the purpofe we find not (in the Tragedy) of this fecond King; fave only when he concludes the Play, and tells us, that he (for his part) will take warning how ever he meddles with a Woman; as before has been cited.

Callianax is an old humorous Lord, neither *wife* nor *valiant*, as himfelf confeffes; and yet is entrufted with the ftrength and keys of the Kingdom: whereas, in Comedy, he would fcarce pafs for a good Yeoman of the Cellar.

His Daughter, *Afpatia*, that gives name to this Tragedy, makes alfo here a very fimple *figure*. Never did *Amintas* or *Paftor fido* know any thing fo tender; nor were the *Arcadian* Hills ever water'd with the tears of a creature fo innocent. Pretty Lamb! how mournfully it bleats! it
needs

needs no *articulate* voice to move our compassion: it seeks no shades but under the *dismal Yew*; and browses only on *Willow-garlands*: yet it can speak for a kiss or so.

> *Asp.* *I'll trouble you no more, yet I will take*
> *A parting kiss, and will not be deny'd.*
> *You'l come, my Lord, and for the Virgins weep*
> *When I am laid in earth; though you your self*
> *Can know no pitty. Thus I wind my self*
> *Into this Willow garland. &c.*

At this rate of tattle she runs on, and never knows when she has said enough.

This *Aspatia* is a Lord's Daughter, and bred at Court; yet is in the presence, and in the Bed-chamber of the Lady that supplants her, and amongst the Bride-maids, where she acts her part; and fawns upon the perjur'd man that forsakes her. And now can-

cannot I be perswaded that there is ought of nature or probability in all this. Much less would I think this a Woman to handle a Sword, and kick *Amintor*, as we see her do soon after. Nor can I conceive wherein consists that *blessing*, as she calls it; which she propos'd to her self, in being kill'd by his hands. This may be *Romance*, but not *Nature*.

And certainly, of all the characters, this of *Amintor* is the most unreasonable. No reason appears why he was contracted to *Aspatia*, and less why he forsook her for *Evadne*; and least of all for his dissembling, and bearing so patiently the greatest of provocations that could possibly be given. Certainly no spectacle can be more displeasing, than to see a man ty'd to a post, and another buffetting him with an immoderate tongue. Certainly nothing can please a generous mind better, than that of *Virgil*.

Parcere subjectis, & debellare superbos.

Poetry

Poetry will allow no provocation or injury, where it allows no revenge. And what pleasure can there be in seeing a King threaten and hector without cause; when none may be suffer'd to make a return? Poetry will not permit an affront, where there can be no reparation. But well was it for us all, that *Amintor* was by the Poet his *maker*, endu'd with a restraining grace, and had his hands ty'd.

The King should first have kill'd his own Mother to have made him mad enough, and fitted him for such a monstrous provocation. And *Amintor* too should have been guilty of some enormous crime, (as he is indeed) that drew this curse upon him, and prepar'd him to receive so horrid an out-rage. Both should have been ripe for punishment, which this occasion pulls down upon them, by making them kill each other. Then *Poetical Justice* might have had its course, though no way could pitty be due to either of them.

But

But surely this character of *Amintor* is (*a*) inconsistent, and is contradiction all over. He is a man of *Honour*, yet breaks his Faith with his Mistress, bears the greatest of affronts from his Wife that ever was given, and dissembles it. 'Tis true; once or twice he is for singing a *Catch*, for the Fiddle and Dancing; but his countenance is not always set after that copy; he does not always dissemble *scurvily*: for sometimes we have him looking so pleas'd, that Comedy would almost be asham'd of such a Cuckold.

He is also honest, and of unshaken loyalty; yet sometimes has such devillish *throws*, as would afright any true *liege* people from sitting at a Coffee-house near him.

And all the *passions* in him work so aukwardly, as if he had *suck'd a Sow*. Thus he threatens.

 Am. ---- *Come to my bed, or by those hairs,*

(*a*) ——— *Servetur ad imum*
Qualis ab incepto processeret, & sibi constet:
         (*Which*

(Which, if thou hadst a Soul like to thy locks,
Were threads for Kings to wear about their arms:
Am. *Why so perhaps they are.)*
Am. *I'l drag thee to my bed.---*

Should not he rather have kick'd her out of doors? And did ever man huff with such a *parenthesis*?

As the *Scene* and provocations work higher; what *Aspatia* might have said to him, he whines to *Evadne.*

Am. *What a strange thing am I?*
Evad. *A miserable one, one that my self am sorry for.*
Am. *Why shew it then in this,*
If thou hast pitty, though thy love is none:
Kill me, and all true Lovers that shall live
In after-ages, crost in their desires,
Shall bless thy memory, and call thee good,

Be-

*Because such mercy in thy heart
 was found
To rid a lingring Wretch.*

Amintor lov'd *Aspatia*, and marri'd *Evadne*, only because the King commanded him. We heard nothing of his love to *Evadne* till now, that he is turn'd the amorous *Owf*, when he ought to be all rage and indignation.

When he should be silenc'd, he falls a preaching.

> Am. *Oh thou hast nam'd a word
> that wipes away
> All thoughts revengeful; in that
> sacred name
> The King, there lies a terror;
> what frail man
> Dares lift his hand against it; let
> the gods
> Speak to him when they please;
> till then let us suffer and wait.*

This is loyal breath; but presently comes a puff that drives us back to the North of *Scotland*.

*Am. ----And it is some ease
To me in these extremes, that I knew this
Before I touch't thee; else had all the sins
Of mankind stood betwixt me and the King,
I had gone through 'em to his heart and thine.*

Oh, says he, 'tis well its no worse, for had I lain with thee, I should have been all fire and fury; I would not have valu'd twenty Kings, but have kill'd 'em all. Well *Amintor, de gustibus non est disputandum,* there is difference betwixt men and men; some one, peradventure, of a grosser sense, might have been as cool and well content, if he had been permitted the honour to *touch* for once where his Majesty had toucht before. But now the storm is over, and he proceeds.

*Am. ----Give me thy hand,
Be careful of thy credit, and sin close,*

'Tis

'Tis all I wish; upon my Chamber-floor
I'le rest to night, that morning visiters
May think we did as married people use,
And prithee smile upon me when they come;
And seem to toy, as if thou hadst been pleas'd
With what we did. *Evad.* Fear not, I will do this.
Am. Come let us practise, and as wantonly
As ever loving Bride and Bride-groom met;
Let's laugh and enter here. *Evad.* I am content.
Am. Down all the swellings of my troubled heart.
When we walk thus entwin'd, let all eyes see,
If ever Lovers better did agree.

See how he concludes too, to the eternal disgrace of *Rhime.* One might think that a man in his *predicament* should scarce be in a mood to be so very

very particular, and enlarge thus upon the subject, unless he were well pleas'd with the occasion. Besides, we find here, *Lovers, entic'd, laugh, Bridegroom, Bride, loving, wantonly, pleas'd, toy, prethee, did as married people use*; so many pleasant words and pretty, got together, *Longinus* would swear that no man could be angry at heart with all these in his mouth; they ought none of them to be nam'd on the same day with *Evadne*, and the transactions in this *Tragedy*. What I have cited, is only from the *first Scene*, wherein *Amintor* has business; nor would I follow him farther, but that in the third *Act*, betwixt him and *Melantius* we find the first occasion for a Tragical passion that yet (I think) these *Plays* have afforded us; which arises from the conduct of an Husband who discovers the secret of his Wives dishonour to his Friend her Brother. *Melantius* importunes *Amintor* to tell the cause of his trouble. When the matter comes to be broken, they proceed thus:

Mel.

Mel. ----*What is it?*
Am. *Why 'tis this, ---it is too big*
To get out, let my tears make way
  awhile.

Here I suppose, *Amintor* might better have wept, without telling it to *Melantius*.

Mel. *Punish me strangely Heaven,*
  if he escape
Of life or fame, that brought this
  Youth to this.
Am. *Your Sister.*
Mel. *Well said.*
Am. *You'l wish't unknown, when*
you have heard it.
Mel. *No.*
Amint. *Is much to blame,*
And to the King has given her Ho-
  nour up---

This line at the full length, is surely enough, his care is, so to mince that matter as not to offend the Brother. Some broken speeches, as *your Sister, the King, her honour,* or the like, with now and then a sprinkling of his tears, might have suffic'd, and the Brother should have been left to guess and paraphrase the broad meaning. But *Amintor* harps upon the same string out of time himself. What follows, is plainly to upbraid and affront his Friend by words, though he intended nothing less; for he goes on:

Am. *And lives in whoredom with him.*

And what yet is more silly, in the next he adds,

Am. *She's wanton, I am loath to say a whore,*
Though it be true.

This provokes *Melantius* to draw his Sword, and he is for fighting *Amintor*; yet I am apt to be of *Amintors* mind, which he thus expresses:

Am. *---It was base in you,*

To

To urge a weighty secret from your Friend,
And then rage at it.

Yet *Melantius* persists, till *Amintor* is provoked to draw his Sword, and then *Melantius* puts up. *Harlequin* and *Scaramouttio* might do these things. Tragedy suffers 'em not, here is no place for Cowards, nor for giddy fellows, and Bullies with their squabbles. When a Sword is once drawn in Tragedy, the Scabbard may be thrown away; there is no leaving what is once design'd, till it be thoroughly effected. *Iphigenia Taurica* went to sacrifice *Orestes*, and she desisted, why? she discover'd him to be her Brother. None here are such Fools as by words to begin a quarrel; nor of so little resolution, to be talkt agen from it, without some new emergent cause that diverts them. No (a) simple alteration of mind ought to produce or hinder any action in a Tragedy.

(a) *Arist.*

Yet far more faulty is what follows; the *counter-turn* has no shadow of sense or sobriety. *Melantius* has swaggered away his fury, and now *Amintor* is all agog to be afighting; for what; but to get his secret back again.

Am. ----*Give it me again,*
Or I will find it wheresoe're it lies
Hid in the mortall'st part, invent
a way to get it back.

Thou art mad *Amintor*, Bedlam is the only place for thee; if thou comest here with thy madness, Tragedy expects (b) *ut cum ratione insanias.*

Hercules was mad, and kill'd his Wife and Children, yet there was reason in his madness; a mist was cast before his eyes, he mistook them for their enemies, and believ'd he was revenging their quarrel whilst he beat their brains out. That was a madness might move pity; but this of *Amintor* is meerly bruitish,

(b) *Terence.*

and

and can move nothing but our aversion. Here is a bluster begun without provocation, and ended without any thing of satisfaction.

But that I may never find a fault without shewing something better. For a quarrel betwixt two friends, with the *turn* and *counter-turn*: let me commend that Scene in the *Iphigenia* in *Aulide*. Where *Agamemnon* having consented that his Daughter should be sacrific'd, and (that her Mother might let her come the more willingly) sent for her with a pretence that she was to be marri d to *Achilles*; yet in a fit of Fatherly tenderness he privately dispatches Letters to hinder her coming. *Menelaus* meets the Messenger going from *Agamemnon*, suspects the business, takes the Letters from him before *Agamemnon*'s face, and read them; and now arose the contest: *Menelaus* was zealous for the publick good, the more, because it agreed so much with his own interest: and *Agamemnon* had cause enough to stand up for his Daughter; but yet, at length, with weep-

weeping eyes, and shame for his weakness and partiality, he yielded up the cause. But *Menelaus* now seeing the conflict of *Agamemnon*, the tears rowling down his cheeks, and his repentance, this sight melted the heart of him, and now he turns Advocate for *Iphigenia:* He will have *Hellen* and the concerns of *Greece* left to the mercy of Heaven, rather than that his Brother *Agamemnon* should do so much violence to himself; and that so vertuous a young Princess be trapan'd to lose her life.

Here all the motions arise from occasions great and just; and this is matter for a *Scene* truly passionate and Tragical.

We may remember (how-ever we find this Scene of *Melanthius* and *Amintor* written in the Book) that at the *Theater* we have a good Scene Acted, there is work cut out, and both our *Æsopus* and *Roscius* are on the Stage together: Whatever defect may be in *Amintor* and *Melanthius*; Mr. *Hart* and Mr. *Mohun* are wanting in nothing. To these we owe for
what

what is pleasing in the Scene; and to this Scene we may impute the success of the *Maids Tragedy*.

The *Drolls* in this *Play* make not so much noise as in the two former; but are less excusable here. In the former they keep some distance, and make a sort of *interlude*: but here they thrust into the principal places; when we should give our full attention to what is Tragedy. When we would listen to a *Lute*, our ears are rapt with the *tintamar* and twang of the *Tongs* and *Jewstrumps*. A man may be free to make a jest of his own misfortunes: but surely 'tis unnatural and barbarous to laugh when we see another on the Scaffold. Some would laugh to find me mentioning *Sacrifices*, *Oracles*, and *Goddesses*: old Superstitions, say they, not practicable, but more than ridiculous on our Stage. These have not observ'd with what Art *Virgil* has manag'd the Gods of *Homer*, nor with what judgment *Tasso* and *Cowley* employ the heavenly powers in a Christian Poem. The like hints from *Sophocles* and *Euripides*

des might also be improv'd by modern Tragedians; and something thence devis'd suitable to our Faith and Customes. 'Tis the general reason I contend for: Nor would I more have Oracles or Goddesses on the Stage, then hear the persons speak *Greek*, they are Apes and not men that imitate with so little discretion.

Some would blame me for insisting and examining only what is apt to *please*, without a word of what might profit.

1. I believe the end of all Poetry is to *please*.

2. Some sorts of Poetry please without profiting.

3. I am confident whoever writes a Tragedy cannot please but must also profit; 'tis the Physick of the mind that he makes palatable.

And besides the *purging* of the *passions*; something must stick by observing that constant order, that harmony and beauty of Providence, that necessary relation and chain, whereby the causes and the effects, the vertues and rewards, the vices and their punish-

punishments are proportion'd and link'd together; how deep and dark foever are laid the Springs, and however intricate and involv'd are their operations.

But thefe enquiries I leave to men of more flegm and confideration.

Othello comes next to hand, but laying my Papers together without more fcribling, I find a volumn, and a greater burthen then I dare well obtrude upon you.

If I blindly wander in erroneous paths, 'tis more then time Mr. *Shepheard* that you fet me right, and if I am not fo much out of the way; then moft of the main faults in thefe other Tragedies cannot be far from our view, if we tread not on their skirts already.

I will wait your direction e're I advance farther, and be fure of your pardon for what is paft. Many feeming contradictions I rather chofe to flip over, then to be ever cafting in your way fome *parenthefis* or fome *diftinction*.

Many

Many other flips and miftakes too you meet withall, but *the fortune of* Greece *depends not on them.*

Nor I know could you (that read Hebrew without the pricks) be at a lofs for the fenfe, where you found not a period truly pointed.

If the Characters I have examin'd are the fame I take them for, I fend you Monfters enough for one *Bartholmew-fair*: but what would vex a Chriftian, thefe are fhown us for our own likeneffes, thefe are the *Duch* Pictures of humane kind.

I have thought our Poetry of the laft Age as rude as our Architecture, one caufe thereof might be, that *Aristotle*'s *treatife of Poetry* has been fo little ftudied amongft us, it was perhaps Commented upon by all the great men in *Italy*, before we well know (on this fide of the *Alps*) that there was fuch a Book in being. And though *Horace* comprizes all in that fmall Epiftle of his; yet few will think long enough together to be Mafters, and to underftand the reafon of what is deliver'd fo in fhort. With

With the remaining *Tragedies* I shall also send you some reflections on that *Paradise lost* of *Miltons*, which some are pleas'd to call a Poem, and assert *Rime* against the slender Sophistry wherewith he attacques it: and also a Narrative of *Petrarch's* Coronation in the *Capitol*, with all the *Pontificalibus* on that occasion, which seems wanting in *Selden*, where he treats on that subject. Let me only anticipate a little in behalf of the *Cataline*, and now tell my thoughts, that though the contrivance and œconomy is faulty enough, yet we there find (besides what is borrow'd from others) more of Poetry and of good thought, more of Nature and of Tragedy, then peradventure can be scrap't together from all those other *Plays*.

Nor can I be displeas'd with honest *Ben*, when he rather chooses to borrow a *Melon* of his Neighbour, than to treat us with a *Pumpion* of his own growth.

But

But all is submitted to you Men of better sense, by

SIR,

Your most obliged humble Servant

T. Rymer.

THE Life of Sir *Walter Raliegh*, with his Trial and Arraignment at *Winchester*, in octavo, price bound 2 s.

Antony and *Cleopatra*, a Tragedy, as it is Acted at the Dukes Theater, written by the Honourable Sir *Charles Sedley*, Baronet, price 1 s.

Circe, a Tragedy, as it is Acted at the Dukes Theater, written by *Charles D'avenant*, L.L.D. price 1 s.

Don Carlos, Prince of *Spain*, a Tragedy, as it is Acted at the Dukes Theater, written by *Tho. Otway*, price 1 s.

The Art of making Love, or Rules for the Conduct of Ladies and Gallants in their Amours, price bound 1 s.

Are sold by *R. Tonson*, at *Grays-Inn* Gate next *Grays-Inn* Lane.

A
Short View
OF
TRAGEDY;

It's *Original, Excellency,* and *Corruption.*

WITH SOME

Reflections on *Shakespear*, and other Practitioners for the STAGE.

By Mr. *Rymer*, Servant to their Majesties.

— *Hodieque manent vestigia ruris.* Hor.

LONDON,

Printed and are to be sold by *Richard Baldwin*, near the *Oxford Arms* in *Warwick-Lane*, and at the *Black Lyon* in *Fleetstreet*, between the two Temple-Gates. 1693.

TO THE
RIGHT HONOURABLE
Charles,
Earl of *Dorset* and *Middle-sex*, Baron *Buckhurst*, and L*d*. *Chamberlain* of their Majesties Houshold, Kt. of the Most Noble Order of the *Garter*, Lord Lieutenant of *Sussex*, and one of their Majesties most Honourable *Privy Council*.

My Lord,

COntemplation and Action have their different Seasons. It was after the defeat of *Antony*, and

The Epistle Dedicatory.

the business of the World pretty well over, when *Virgil* and *Horace* came to be so distinguish'd at Court.

Alexander, who had given so good proof of his Judgment by the Honours paid to the Memory of *Homer*, and of *Pindar*, found in his time no better Poet than *Chærilus*. *Chærilus* to the great *Alexander*, was for *Laureate* and *Historiographer*.

When once again the business of the World is over, Now my Lord, that the *Muses* Commonweal is become your Province, what may we not expect? This I say, not with intent to apply that of *Quintilian* on *Augustus Cæsar*, *Parum Diis visum est esse eum Maximum Poetarum*: that were a Common Topick: But because, when some years ago, I tryed the Publick with Observations concerning the Stage; It was principally your Countenance that buoy'd me

up,

The Epistle Dedicatory.

up, and supported a Righteous Cause against the Prejudice and Corruption then reigning.

I would not raise up again the Spirit of the late Prince of *Conti*; His *Traitè contre la Comedie*, has by others been termed *la defense de la vertu*. My zeal goes no higher than the Doctrine of *Horace*, and *Aristotle*; and the Primitive Fathers of *Dramatick Poetry*: If that Purity may be Allow'd under a Christian Dispensation.

The World, surely, other Matters apart, owes much to Cardinal *Richelieu*, for his Encouragement to the *Belles Lettres*. From thence we may reckon, that we begin to understand the Epick Poem by the means of *Bossu*; and Tragedy by Monsieur *Dacier*. The World is not agreed which is the Nobler Poem: *Plato* and *Bossu* prefer the for-

The Epistle, &c.

former; *Aristotle* and *Dacier* declare for Tragedy. Three, indeed, of the Epick (the two by *Homer* and *Virgil*'s *Æneids*) are reckon'd in the degree of Perfection: But amongst the Tragedies, only the *Oedipus* of *Sophocles*. That, by *Corneille*, and by others, of a Modern Cut, *quantum Mutatus*! but I already trespass too long upon your time, who am,

My Lord,

Your ever Bounden Faithful

Humble Servant.

THE

Contents.

Chap. I. *The* Chorus *keeps the Poet to Rules. A* show *to the Spectators. Two Senses to be pleased. The* Eye, *by the* Show, *and by the* Action. *Plays Acted without words. Words often better out of the way. Instances in* Shakespear. Ben Johnson *and* Seneca *Noted. To the* Ear, Pronunciation *is all in all. The Story of* Demosthenes. *Mistakes in Judging. Two sorts of Judges. At* Athens *a Third sort. Judges upon Oath. In* France *Judges divided about the* Cid. *Cardinal* Richelieu *against the* Majority. *At the* Thomas Morus, *weeping unawares.* Horace *Angry with* Shows. *The* French Opera *inconsistent with Nature and Good sense. Burlesk Verse. At* Paris *Christ's Passion in Burlesk. A Tragedy of* Aeschylus. *The defeat of* Xerxes. *The Subject, and Oeconomy. How imitated for our* English *Stage. King* John *of* France,
Francis

The Contents.

Francis 1. *Prisoners. The* Spanish *Armado in* 88. *An imitation, recommended to Mr.* Dreyden.

Chap. 2. Tragedy *before* Thespis. *A Religious Worship:* Musick *and* Dance *follow the* Chorus: *Governments care of the Stage, as of Religion. No Private Person to build a Chappel. Young Men not to present Plays.* Didascalia, *and* Tragedy-doctors. *Difficulty. Publick Revenue for Plays. Theatre-money sacred. End of Poetry. What effect by* Aeschylus. *Of his Persians. Schools for Boys. Stage for Men. Character of* Aristophanes. *Opinion of the Persian Ambassador. The State takes aim from him. Spares not his Master the* People. *Democratical Corruption. His Address unimitable.* Comedy *after him dwindles. Somewhat like him amongst the Moderns. Rehearsal; Alchymist. Vertuoso. Rabilais.*

End of Poetry with the Romans. *Tragedies by their Great Men. All Translation.* Numa Pompilius. *Old* Romans *aversion to Poetry.* 12 *Tables. Stage-Plays to remove the Plague. Never improv'd by them. The use hardly known. Far short of the* Greeks. Horace *and* Virgil. *Their Conduct.* Terence's *Complaint. Wanted Show. And Action.* Athens *the Soil for Dramatick Poetry. A forreign Plant with the* Romans. *They for the Eye, pleas'd more with the*

The Contents.

the outside. Their Theatres considerable, not the Tragedies. Horace's *Reason.*

Chap. 3. *The first Christians cry against Idols, Stage-Plays, Pagan Worship. Apostolical Constitutions.* Greek *and* Latin *Fathers.* Tertullian's *Conceipt. Counsels against* Heathen *Learning.* Greek-Wisdom. St. Hierom, St. Austin, *their Sin of* Heathen *Books. A Canon that no Bishop read an* Heathen *Book. Julians Project. The Christians Countermine. A Christian* Homer, Pindar, *and* Euripides. *Stage-Plays particularly level'd at. The same heat at this day in the* Spanish Jesuits. Pedro de Guzman *against Stage-Plays and Bull-feasts. The Name of Poet a Bugbear at the Reformation. The Heresie charged on Sing-Songs, and Stage-plays.* Marot's *Psalms. How in vogue at the* French-Court. *Reasons against Stage-plays.* Lactantius. *The same* 2000 *years ago by* Plato. *Tragedy,* Homer, Aeschylus. *Objections by* Aristophanes.

Chap. 4:

The Contents.

Chap. 4. Aristotle's *general Answer evasive.* Plato *a better Divine. Not better than our Modern.* God *may use ill instruments. The false Dream. The two Barrels. Fables before* Homer. *He of God sensibly.* Plato, Cant. *Metaphore the utmost we are capable of. Fables. Allegory.* Celsus *to* Origen *against the Bible. Allegory, a cure for all.* Homer's *Fables from the Bible. The false Dream, from the Story of* Achab *improv'd by* Homer. Averroes *of* Arabian *Poets.* Apollo Loxias. *Particular sentences. Texts of Scripture.* Juno, Job's Wife. SS. *in Vulgar Tongue.* Euripides, *ill Women. No blame to the art. Pomp of the Theatre. What ill names by* Jesuits.

Chap. 5. *Of Poetry in* Italy. Aristotle's *Works.* Tramontains. *Cardinal* Bibiena. *Tragedy there with* Chorus. Strolers. Christ's Passion.

Of Poetry in France. Clem. Marot. Strolers *there. Proceedings at Law against them. Report of their Case. Their* Old Testament. *Acts of the* Apostles, *and* Christ's Passion. *Banisht from* France. *Comedy there. Tragedy by* Hardy, Corneille, Richilieu. *Academy Royal. The Theatre. Caution that no* Equivoque, *nor ought against good Manners.*

The Contents.

ners. More nice than the Pulpit. Their Gallantry, Verse, Language, unfit for Tragedy. Dramatick representations banish'd from Spain. Nurse of Heresie. Father Guzman. Escobar.

Of Poetry in England. *British, Saxon, Norman, Latin and* Provencial *Poetry there.* Richard Ceur de Lion, *a* Provencial *Poet. Our Monks and History false on that account. The* Gay Science. *That and the* Albigenses *Contemporary, and from the same Country.* King Richard's *Fellow-Poets.* Jeffry Rudel, *and Countess of* Tripoly.

Chap. 6. Savery de Mauleon *a Provencial Poet. Testimony of him. King* R. I. *His Verses when Prisoner in* Austria. *The Emperor* Frederick Barbarossa. *His Poetry.* Ramond Beringhier. *Four Daughters, four Queens.* Rob. Grosthead. *His Provencial Poetry. Other Languages stubborn.* Chaucer *refin'd our English. Which in perfection by* Waller. *His Poem on the Navy Royal, beyond all modern Poetry in any Language. Before him our Poets better expressed their thoughts in Latin. Whence* Hoveden *might mistake, and his Malice. A Translation from* Grosthead. *The Harp a Musick then in fashion. Five Tragedies from* Joan *Queen of* Naples. *Forreigners all call'd French. Plays by the Parish-Clerks*

The Contents.

Clerks of London. *What under* H. VIII. *flourish under Queen* Elizabeth. *The* Gorboduck. *French much behind-hand with us. Tragedy, with us, but a shadow.*

Chap. 7. Othello. *More of a piece. In Tragedy four parts.* Fable, *the Poets part.* Cinthio's *Novels.* Othello *altered for the worse. Marriage, absurd, forbidden by* Horace. *Fable of* Othello. *Use and Application.* Othello's *Love-powder. High-German Doctor.* Venetians *odd taste of things. Their Women fools. Employ Strangers. Hate the Moors.* Characters. *Nothing of the Moor in* Othello, *of a Venetian in* Desdemona. *Of a Souldier in* Jago. *The Souldiers Character, by* Horace. *What by* Shakespear. Agamemnon. *Venetians no sense of Jealousie.* Thoughts, *in* Othello, *in a Horse, or Mastiff, more sensibly exprest. Ill Manners. Outragious to a Nobleman, to Humanity. Address, in telling bad news. In Princes Courts. In* Aristophanes. *In* Rabelais. *Venetian Senate. Their Wisdom.*

Chap. 8.

The Contents.

Chap. 8. *Reflections on the* Julius Cæsar. *Men famous in History. To be rob'd of their good name, Sacriledge.* Shakespear, *abuse of History. Contradiction, in the character of* Brutus. Villon *and* Dante, *that Hugh Capet from a Butcher. Preparation in Poetry. Strong reasons in* Cassius. *Roman Senators, impertinent as the Venetian.* Portia *as* Desdemona. *The same parts and good breeding. How talk of Business. Whispers.* Brutus's *Tinder-box, Sleepy Boy, Fiddle.* Brutus *and* Cassius, *Flat-foot Mimicks. The Indignity.* Laberius. *Play of the Incarnation. The* Madonna's—*Shouting and Battel. Strolers in* Cornwal. *Rehearsal, law for acting it once a week.*

The Catiline *by* Ben. Johnson. *Why an Orator to be,* vir bonus. *Ben cou'd distinguish Men and Manners.* Sylla's Ghost: *The speech not to be made in a blind Corner.* Corneille. *Common sence teaches Unity of Action. The* Chorus, *of necessity, keep the Poet to time, and place. No rule observ'd. A Life in* Plutarch. *Acts of the Apostles.* Ben *is* fidus interpres. *Is the Horse in Mill in flat opposition to* Horace. *Trifling tale, or corruption of History, unfit for Tragedy. In contempt of Poetry.* Aristophanes, *not the occasion of the Death of* Socrates. *Was for a reformation in the service book. With what address he effected it.*

Sarpen-

The Contents.

Sarpedon's Fast, of divine institution. The least sally from, or Parenthesis in the ancient Comedy of more moment than all our Tragedies. English Comedy the best.

Extrait des Registres du Parlement du Vendredy 9. Decembre l'an 1541. Monsieur de S. André President.

CHAP.

ERRATA.

Page 8. l. 10. Bam
p. 10. l. 5. ingenieuses.
p. 21. l. 20. habergeons.

CHAP. I.

The CONTENTS.

The Chorus keeps the Poet to Rules. A show to the Spectators. Two Senses *to be pleased. The Eye, by the* Show, *and by the* Action. *Plays Acted without Words. Words often better out of the way. Instances in* Shakespear. Ben. Johnson *and* Seneca *Noted. To the* Ear, *Pronunciation is all in all. The Story of* Demosthenes. *Mistakes in Judging. Two sorts of Judges. At* Athens *a Third sort. Judges upon Oath. In* France *Judges divided about the* Cid. *Cardinal* Richelieu *against the Majority. At the* Thomas Morus, *weeping unawares.* Horace *Angry with Shows. The* French *Opera inconsistent with Nature and Good sense. Burlesk Verse. At* Paris Christ's Passion *in Burlesk. A Tragedy of* Aeschylus. *The defeat of* Xerxes. *The Subject, and Oeconomy. How imitated for our* English *Stage. King* John *of* France, Francis 1. *Prisoners. The Spanish Armado in* 88. *An imitation, recommended to Mr.* Dreyden.

WHAT Reformation may not we expect now, that in *France* they see the necessity of a *Chorus* to their Tragedies? *Boyer,* and *Racine,* both of the Royal Academy, have led the Dance; they have tried the success in the last Plays that were Presented by them.

The *Chorus* was the root and original, and is certainly always the most necessary part of Tragedy.

The *Spectators* thereby are secured, that their Poet shall not juggle, or put upon them in the matter of *Place*, and *Time*, other than is just and reasonable for the representation.

And the *Poet* has this benefit; the *Chorus* is a goodly *Show*, so that he need not ramble from his Subject out of his Wits for some foreign Toy or Hobby-horse, to humor the Multitude.

(a) *Aristotle* tells us of *Two Senses* that must be pleas'd, our *Sight*, and our *Ears*: And it is in vain for a *Poet* (with *Bays* in the Rehearsal) to complain of Injustice, and the wrong Judgment in his *Audience*, unless these *Two senses* be gratified.

The worst on it is, that most People are wholly led by these *Two senses*, and follow them upon content, without ever troubling their Noddle farther.

How many Plays owe all their success to a rare *Show*? Even in the days of *Horace*, enter on the Stage a Person in a *Costly strange Habit*, Lord! *What Clapping, what Noise* and Thunder, as Heaven and Earth were coming together! yet not one word spoken.

(a) Poetica.

Dixit

Dixit adhuc aliquid? nil, sane, quid placit Ergo?
Lana Terentino violas imitata veneno

Was there ought said? troth, no, What then did touch ye?
Some Prince of *Bantham*, or a *Mamamouche*.

It matters not whether there be any *Plot*, any *Characters*, any *Sense*, or a wise *Word* from one end to the other, provided in our Play we have the *Senate* of *Rome*, the *Venetian Senate* in their Pontificalibus, or a *Blackamoor* Ruffian, or *Tom Dove*, or other Four-leg'd Hero of the Bear-Garden.

The *Eye* is a quick sense, will be in with our Fancy, and prepossess the Head strangely. Another means whereby the *Eye* misleads our Judgment is the *Action*: We go to see a Play *Acted*; in Tragedy is represented a Memorable *Action*; so the Spectators are always pleas'd to see *Action*, and are not often so ill-natur'd to pry into, and examine whether it be Proper, Just, Natural, in season, or out of season. *Bays* in the Rehearsal well knew this secret: The *Two Kings* are at their *Coranto*; nay, the *Moon and the Earth* dance the *Hey*; any thing in Nature, or against Nature, rather than allow the *Serious Councel*, or other dull business to interrupt, or obstruct *Action*.

(4)

This thing of *Action* finds the blindside of humane-kind an hundred ways. We laugh and weep with those that laugh or weep; we gape, stretch, and are very *dotterels* by example.

Action is speaking to the Eyes; and all *Europe* over Plays have been represented with great applause, in a Tongue unknown, and sometimes without any Language at all.

Many, peradventure, of the Tragical Scenes in *Shakespear*, cry'd up for the *Action*, might do yet better without words: Words are a sort of heavy baggage, that were better out of the way, at the push of Action; especially in his *bombast Circumstance*, where the Words and Action are seldom akin, generally are inconsistent, at cross purposes, embarrass or destroy each other; yet to those who take not the words distinctly, there may be something in the buz and sound, that like a drone to a Bagpipe may serve to set off the *Action*: For an instance of the former, Would not a rap at the door better express *Jago*'s meaning? than

―――― *Call aloud.*

Jago. *Do with like timerous accent, and dire yel,*

As

As when by night and negligence the fire
Is spied in populous Cities.

For, What Ship? Who is Arrived? The Answer is,

'Tis one Jago, *Auncient to the General,*
He has had most Favourable and Happy
  speed;
Tempests themselves, high Seas, and houling
  Winds,
The guttered Rocks, and congregated Sands,
Traytors ensteep'd, to clog the guiltless Keel,
As having sense of Beauty, do omit
Their common Natures, letting go safely by
The divine Desdemona.

Is this the Language of the Exchange, or the Ensuring-Office? Once in a man's life, he might be content at *Bedlam* to hear such a rapture. In a Play one should speak like a man of business, his speech must be Πολιτικός, which the *French* render *Agissante*; the *Italians*, *Negotiosa*, and *Operativa*; but by this Gentleman's talk one may well guess he has nothing to do. And he has many Companions, that are

———*Hey day!*
I know not what to do, nor what to say. (*b*)

(*b*) Rehearsal.

It was then a ſtrange imagination in *Ben. Johnſon*, to go ſtuff out a Play with *Tully*'s Orations. And in *Seneca*, to think his dry Morals, and a tedious train of Sentences might do feats, or have any wonderful operation in the *Drama*.

Some go to *ſee*, others to *hear* a Play. The Poet ſhould pleaſe both; but be ſure that the *Spectators* be ſatisfied, whatever Entertainment he give his *Audience*.

But if neither the *Show*, nor the *Action* cheats us, there remains ſtill a notable vehicle to carry off nonſenſe, which is the *Pronunciation*.

By the loud Trumpet, which our Courage aids;
We learn, That ſound, as well as ſenſe perſwades. (c)

Demoſthenes (d) had a good ſtock of Senſe, was a great Maſter of Words; could turn a period, and draw up his tropes in a line of Battel; and fain would he have ſeen ſome effect of his Orations; no body was mov'd, no body minded him. He goes to the Playhouſe, bargains with an Actor, and learn'd of him to ſpeak Roundly and Gracefully: From that time, Who but *Demoſthenes*? Never ſuch a leading man! whenever he ſpake, no diviſion,

(c) Waller. (d) Plutarch, Demoſthen.

not

not a vote to the contrary, the whole House were with him, *Nemine Contradicente*. This change observ'd, a Friend went to him for the secret; Tell me, says he, your *Nostrum*, tell me your Receipt; What is the main Ingredient that makes an Orator? *Demosthenes* answered, *Pronunciation*: What then the next thing? *Pronunciation:* Pray then, What the Third? Still the answer was *Pronunciation*.

Now this was at *Athens*, where want of Wit was never an objection against them. So that it is not in *Song* only, that a *good voice* diverts us from the Wit and Sense. From the Stage, the Bar or the Pulpit, a *good voice* will prepossess our ears, and having seized that Pass, is in a fair way to surprise our Judgment.

Considering then what power the *Show*, the *Action*, and the *Pronunciation* have over us, it is no wonder that wise men often mistake, and give an hasty Judgment, which upon a review is justly set aside.

Horace divides the *Judges* into *Majores Numero*, and the few or *better sort*; and these for the most part were of different Judgments: The like distinction may hold in all other Nations; only at *Athens* there was a third sort, who were Judges upon (*f*) Oath,

(*f*) Plutarch, *Cimon*.

Judges in Commission, by the Government sworn to do right, and determine the Merits of a Play, without favour or affection.

But amongst the Moderns, never was a Cause canvass'd with so much heat, between the Play-Judges, as that in *France*, about *Corneille*'s Tragedy of the *Cid*. The Majority were so fond of it, that with them it became a Proverb, (*f*) *Cela est plus beau que la Cid.* On the other side, Cardinal *Richelien* damn'd it, and said, *All the pudder about it, was only between the ignorant people, and the men of judgment.*

Yet this Cardinal with so nice a taste, had not many years before been several times to see acted the Tragedy of Sir *Thomas Moor*, and as often wept at the Representation. Never were known so many people (*g*) crowded to death, as at that Play. Yet was it the Manufacture of *Jehan de Serre*, one about the form of our *Flekno*, or *Thomas Jordan*. The same *de Serre*, that dedicated a Book of Meditations to K. *Charles* I. and went home with Pockets full of Medals and Reward.

By this Instance we see a man the most sharp, and of the greatest penetration was imposed upon by these cheating Sences,

(*f*) Pelisson. *Hist. Acad.*   (*g*) *Parnasse Reform.*

the Eyes and the Ears, which greedily took in the impreſſion from the *Show*, the *Action*, and from the Emphaſis and *Pronunciation*; tho there was no great matter of *Fable*, no *Manners*, no fine *Thoughts*, no *Language*; that is, nothing of a Tragedy, nothing of a Poet all the while.

Horace was very angry with theſe empty *Shows* and Vanity, which the Gentlemen of his time ran like mad after.

----Inſanos oculos, et gaudia vana.

What woud he have ſaid to the *French Opera* of late ſo much in vogue? There it is for you to bewitch your *eyes*, and to charm your *ears*. There is a Cup of Enchantment, there is Muſick and Machine; *Circe* and *Calipſo* in conſpiracy againſt Nature and good Senſe. 'Tis a Debauch the moſt inſinuating, and the moſt pernicious; none would think an *Opera* and Civil Reaſon, ſhould be the growth of one and the ſame Climate. But ſhall we wonder at any thing for a Sacrifice to the *Grand Monarch*? ſuch Worſhip, ſuch Idol. All flattery to him is inſipid, unleſs it be prodigious: Nothing reaſonable, or within compaſs can come near the Matter. All muſt be monſtrous, enormous, and outragious to Nature, to be like him, or give any Eccho on his Appetite.

Were

Were *Rabelais* alive again, he would look on his *Garagantua* as but a Pygmy.

(h)--*The Heroes Race excels the Poets Thought*.
The Academy Royal may pack up their Modes and Methods, *& penses ingenienses*; the *Racines* and the *Corneilles* must all now dance to the Tune of *Baptista*. Here is the *Opera*; here is *Machine* and *Baptista*, farewell *Apollo* and the Muses.

Away with your *Opera* from the Theatre, better had they become the *Heathen* Tepmles; for the *Corybantian Priests*, and (*Semiviros Gallos*) the old *Capons* of *Gaul*, than a People that pretend from *Charlemayn*, or descend from the undoubted Loyns of *Germain* and *Norman* Conquerors.

In the *French*, not many years before was observed the like vicious appetite, and immoderate Passion for *vers Burlesque*.

They were currant in *Italy* an hundred years, ere they passed to this side the *Alps*; But when once they had their turn in *France*, so right to their humour, they over-ran all; (*i*) nothing wise or sober might stand in their way. All were possessed with the Spirit of *Burlesk*, from *Doll* in the Dairy, to the Matrons at Court, and Maids of Honour. Nay, so far went the

(*h*) Waller. (i) *Pelisson Histor. Acad.*

Frenzy,

Frenzy, that no Bookseller wou'd meddle on any terms without *Burlesk*; insomuch that *Ann.* 1649. was at *Paris* printed a serious Treatise with this Title,

----La Passion de Nostre Seigneur, En vers Burlesques.

If we cannot rise to the Perfection of intreigue in *Sophocles*, let us sit down with the honesty and simplicity of the first beginners in Tragedy: As for example;

One of the most simple now extant, is the *Persians* by *Aeschylus*.

Some ten years after that Darius *had been beaten by the* Greeks, Xerxes *(his Father* Darius *being dead) brought against them such Forces by Sea and Land, the like never known in History:* Xerxes *went also in person, with all the* Maison de Roy, Satrapie *and* Gendarmery; *all were routed.* Some forty years afterwards the Poet takes hence his subject for a Tragedy.

The Place *is by* Darius's *Tomb, in the Metropolis of* Persia.

The Time *is the Night, an hour or two before day break.*

First, on the Stage are seen 15 *Persons in Robes, proper for the Satrapa, or Chief Princes in* Persia: *Suppose they met so early at the Tomb, then sacred, and ordinarily resorted*

to

(12)

to by people troubled in mind, on the accounts of Dreams, or any thing not boding good. They talk of the state of Affairs: Of Greece *; and of the Expedition. After some time take upon them to be the* Chorus.

The next on the Stage comes Atossa *the Queen Mother of* Persia *; she cou'd not lie in Bed for a Dream that troubled her ; so in a fit of Devotion comes to her Husband's Tomb, there luckily meets with so many Wise-men and Counsellors to ease her Mind by interpreting her Dream ; This with the* Chorus *makes the Second Act.*

After this, their Disorder, Lamentation and Wailing, is such, that Darius *is disturbed in his Tomb, so his Ghost appears, and belike stays with them till Day-break : Then the* Chorus *concludes the Act.*

In the Fourth Act come the Messengers with sad Tidings, which, with the reflections and troubles thereupon, and the Chorus, *fill out this Act.*

In the Last, Xerxes *himself arrives, which gives occasion of condoling, houling, and distraction enough, to the end of the Tragedy.*

One may imagine how a *Grecian* Audience that lov'd their Countrey, and glory'd in the Vertue of their Ancestors wou'd be affected with this Representation.

Never

Never appeared on the Stage a Ghost of greater consequence. The *Grand Monarch Darius*, who had been so shamefully beaten by those petty Provinces of the United *Grecians*, could not now lye quiet in his Grave for them; but must be raised from the dead again, to be witness of his Son's Disgrace, and of their Triumph.

Were a Tragedy after this Model to be drawn for our Stage, *Greece* and *Persia* are too far from us: The Scene must be laid nearer home: As at the *Louvre*; and instead of *Xerxes* we might take *John*, King of *France*, and the Battel of *Poictiers*. So if the *Germans* or *Spaniards* were to compose a Play, on the Battel of *Pavia*, and King *Francis* there taken Prisoner, the Scene shou'd not be laid at *Vienna*, or at *Madrid*, but at the *Louvre*. For there the Tragedy wou'd principally operate, and there all the Lines most naturally centre.

But perhaps the memorable Adventure of the *Spaniards* in 88. against *England*, may better resemble that of *Xerxes*: Suppose then a Tragedy call'd The *Invincible Armado*.

The Place, *then for the Action, may be at* Madrid, *by some* Tomb, *or solemn place of resort; or if we prefer a Turn in it from good to bad Fortune, then some* Drawing-Room *in the Palace near the King's Bed-chamber.*

The

The Time *to begin, Twelve at Night.*

The Scene opening presents 15 *Grandees of* Spain, *with their most solemn Beards and Accoutrements, met there (suppose) after some Ball, or other publick occasion. They talk of the state of Affairs, the greatness of their Power, the vastness of their Dominions, and prospect to be infallibly, ere long, Lords of all. With this prosperity and goodly thoughts transported, they at last form themselves into the Chorus, and walk such measures, with Musick, as may become the gravity of such a Chorus.*

Then enter two or three of the Cabinet Councel, who now have leave to tell the Secret; That the Preparations and the Invincible Armado was to conquer England. *These, with part of the Chorus, may communicate all the Particulars, the Provisions, and the Strength by Sea and Land; the certainty of success, the Advantages by that accession; and the many Tun of Tar-Barrels for the Hereticks. These Topicks may afford matter enough, with the Chorus, for the Second Act.*

In the Third Act, these Gentlemen of the Cabinet cannot agree about sharing the Preferments of England, *and a mighty broil there is amongst them. One will not be content unless he is King of* Man; *another will be Duke of* Lancaster. *One, that had seen a Coronation in* England, *will by all means be Duke of* Aquitayn,

quitayn, *or elſe Duke of* Normandy. And on this occaſion two Competitors have a juſter occaſion to work up, and ſhew the Muſcles of their Paſſion, then *Shakeſpear's Caſſius* and *Brutus*. *After, the Chorus.*

The Fourth Act may, inſtead of Atoſſa, *preſent ſome old Dames of the Court, us'd to dream Dreams, and to ſee Sprights, in their Night-Rails, and Forhead-Cloaths, to alarm our Gentlemen with new apprehenſions, which make diſtraction and diſorders ſufficient to furniſh out this Act.*

In the laſt Act the King enters, and wiſely diſcourſes againſt Dreams and Hobgoblins, to quiet their minds: And the more to ſatisfie them, and take off their fright, he lets them to know that *St.* Loyala *had appeared to him, and aſſured him that all is well. This ſaid, comes a Meſſenger of the ill News; his Account is lame, ſuſpected, he ſent to Priſon. A ſecond Meſſenger, that came away long after, but had a ſpeedier Paſſage, his account is diſtinct, and all their loſs credited. So in fine, one of the Chorus concludes with that of* Euripides: Thus you ſee the Gods bring things to paſs often, otherwiſe than was by man propoſed.

In this Draught we ſee the Fable, and the Characters or Manners of *Spaniards*, and room for fine Thoughts, and noble Expreſſions, as much as the Poet can afford.

The First Act gives a Review, or Oſtentation of their Strength in Battel-array.

In the Second, they are in motion for the Attack, and we ſee where the Action falls.

In the Third they quarrel about dividing the Spoil.

In the Fourth, They meet with a Repulſe; are beaten off by a Van-Guard of Dreams, Goblins, and Terrors of the Night.

In the Fifth, They rally under their King in Perſon, and make good their Ground, till overpowered by freſh Troops of Conviction; and mighty Truth prevails.

For the Firſt Act, a Painter would draw *Spain* hovering, and ready to ſtrike at the Univerſe.

In the Second, juſt taking *England* in her Pounces.

But it muſt not be forgotten in the Second Act, that there be ſome *Spaniſh-Fryar* or *Jeſuit*, as St. *Xaviere* (for he may drop in by miracle, any where) to ring in their ears *the Northern Hereſie*; like *Jago* in *Shakeſpear*, *Put Money in thy Purſe*, I ſay, *Put Money in thy Purſe*. So often may he repeat *the Northern Hereſie*. Away with your Secular Advantages; *I ſay, the Northern Hereſie*; there is Roaſt-meat for the Church; *Voto a Chriſto, the Northern Hereſie*.

If

If Mr. *Dryden* might try his Pen on this Subject, doubtless, to an Audience that heartily love their Countrey, and glory in the Vertue of their Ancestors, his imitation of *Aschylus* would have better success, and would *Pit*, *Box* and *Gallery*, far beyond any thing now in possession of the Stage, however wrought up by the unimitable *Shakespear*.

CHAP. II.

The CONTENTS.

Tragedy *before* Thespis. *A Religious Worship*: Musick *and* Dance *follow the* Chorus: *Governments care of the Stage, as of Religion. No Private Person to build a Chappel. Young men not to present Plays.* Didascalia, *and* Tragedy-doctors. *Difficulty. Publick Revenue for Plays. Theatre-money sacred. End of Poetry. What effect by* Aeschylus. *Of his* Persians. *Schools for Boys. Stage for Men. Character of* Aristophanes. *Opinion of the* Persian *Ambassador. The State takes aim from him. Spares not his Master the* People. *Democratical Corruption. His Address unimitable.* Comedy *after him dwindles. Somewhat like him amongst the Moderns. Rehearsal.* Alchymist. Vertuoso. Rabilais.

End of Poetry with the Romans. *Tragedies by their Great Men. All Translation.* Numa Pompilius. *Old* Romans *aversion to Poetry.* 12 Tables. *Stage-Plays to remove the Plague. Never improv'd by them. The use hardly known. Far short of the* Greeks. Horace *and* Virgil. *Their Conduct.* Terence's *Complaint. Wanted Show. And Action.* Athens *the Soil for Dramatick Poetry. A forreign Plant with the* Romans. *They for the Eye, pleas'd more with the outside. Their Theatres considerable, not the Tragedies.* Horace's *Reason.*

Authors generally look no higher than *Thespis* for the Original of *Tragedy*; yet *Plato* reckons it much ancienter.

Minos, (a) says he, for all his wisdom, was

(*a*) Minos *dial.*

over-

overseen in making war upon *Athens*; where lived so many Tragic Poets, that represented him, and fixed on him and his Family a Name and Character never to be wiped off.

The *Judges of Hell*, *Pasiphae*, and her *Minotaur*, are upon record to all Posterity.

All agree, that in the beginning it was purely a Religious *Worship*, and solemn Service for their *Holy-days*. Afterwards it came from the *Temples* to the *Theatre*, admitted of a Secular Allay, and grew to be some Image of the World, and Humane Life. When it was brought to the utmost perfection by *Sophocles*, the *Chorus* continued a necessary part of the *Tragedy*; but that Musick and the Dancing which came along with the *Chorus*, were meer Religion, were no part of the *Tragedy*, nor had any thing of Philosophy or Instruction in them.

The *Government* had the same care of these Representations, as of their Religion, and as much caution about them. The Laws would not permit a private person to make a Chappel, raise an Altar, or consecrate an Image; otherwise all places would in time be so cramm'd from the Devotion of Women and weak heads, that a man should not set a foot, nor find elbow-room, for Gods, and Shrines, consecrated stuff.

The like providence had they for the Theatre. No (b) *Poet* under the age of 30 or 40 years was allow'd to present any Play to be acted. *Seldens* Marmora, and other Chronologers inform us that *Aeschylus* had the victory, when he was 40 years old: And *Euripides* not till he was 43. The dramatick Poet was styled *Comædodidascalus*, and *Tragædodidasculus*, as one should say, *Comedy-doctor*, and *Tragedy-doctor*: We find too the Word *didascalia*, with the Titles of *Terence*'s Comedies, which afterwards the *Latins* came to imitate, as *Cicero* in *Brut. Livius qui primus fabulam Docuit*, And *Hor. ---vel qui Docuere Togatæ*. So to write a Play, in the opinion of *Aristophanes*, *Comodc-didascalia*, *is of all things the most difficult*.

More (c) of their publick money was spent about the *Chorus*, and other charges and decorations of their Theatre, than in all their Wars with the Kings of *Persia*.

And when brought to their last extremity, that no other Bank remain'd for them, wherewith to carry on a War, without which War they could not longer expect to be a People, the delicate turn us'd by *Demosthenes*, in starting the motion, for applying this *Theatre-money* to the War, is observ'd as a (d) Masterpiece of address by the Orators. *Did I say* (quoth *Demosthenes*) *the* The-

(b) *Schol.* Aristo.   (c) Demitr. *Libanius.*

atre-money *may be applied to the War? no, by* Jove, *not I.*

Monasteries and Church Lands were never with us so sacred.

In the days of *Aristophanes*, it was on all hands agreed, that the best *Poet* was he who had done the most to make men vertuous and serviceable to the Publick. *In a Dialogue of the dead,* (e) where they dispute the precedence, says *Aeschylus*, *Consider what sort of men I left you.*

Men generous, four Cubits high, not such as now-a-days,

That slip the collar when they should serve their Countrey.

Indifferent, loose (f) *prudential,* (g) *tricking Fellows;*

Nought did they breathe, but broad Swords, Battle-Axes,

The Helmets lofty pride, (h) *Jack-Boots, Hageons,*

With true (i) *Beef-courage.*

So when his *Princes at Thebes*, and when his *Persians* were acted, not a Spectator, but bit his Thumbs with impatience for the Field, to give the Enemy Battel. So his *Patroclus*, his *Tencer*, and his *Thimaleon*'s were represented only to spur on his Coun-

(e) Aristoph. *Frogs.* (f) Κοβάλυς (g) Πανυργυς
(h) κνημῖδας (i) θυμὺς ἐσπαβοεὶυς.

trey-men to Vertue, and provoke them to a generous Emulation.

And here *Aristophanes* declares another Rule (which *Plato* takes from him) That if any thing looks with an ill face, the Poet must hide it; not suffer it, by any means, to be shown or represented in a Play: Because as the Schools are for teaching Children, the Stage should be for men of riper years and Judgment. So that a *Poet* must be sure that his *Doctrine* be good and wholsome.

This Author appears in his Function, a man of wonderful zeal for Vertue, and the good of his Countrey; and he laid about him with an undaunted resolution, as it were some Christian Martyr, for his Faith and Religion. He plainly *ran a Muck* at all manner of Vice where-ever he saw it, be it in the greatest Philosophers, the greatest Poets, the Generals, or the Ministers of State.

The *Persian* Ambassador, who was Lieger there (as formerly the *French* with us) seeing the Town all at his beck; and the Government taking aim, turning out, disgracing, impeaching, banishing, out-lawing and attainting the great men, according as he hinted, or held up the finger, the Ambassador, not understanding the *Atheni*-
tempe

(23)

temper, was aſtoniſh'd at the man.

And, for all the Democracy, no leſs bold was he with his Sovereign, Legiſlative-people: Repreſenting (k) them, taking Bribes, ſelling their Votes, bought off; Nay, the whole Houſe led away for (l) a Diſh of Sprats, or penny-worth of Coriander.

*—— ὥϛε βυλήν ὅλην
ὀβολᾶ κοριάννοις ἀναλαβὼν ἐλήλυθα.*

He tells 'em (as the practice amongſt them) that the Government had no occaſion for men of wit or honeſty. The moſt ignorant, the moſt impudent, and the greateſt Rogue ſtood faireſt always for a Place, and the beſt qualified to be their chief Miniſter. He tells them, nothing ſhall fright him; Truth and Honeſty are on his ſide; he has *the heart of* Hercules, will ſpeak what is juſt and generous, tho *Cerberus*, and all the kennel of Hell-hounds were loo'd upon him.

But then his Addreſs was admirable: He would make the Truth viſible and palpable, and every way ſenſible to them. The Art and the Application; his ſtrange Fetches, his lucky Starts; his odd Inventions, the wild Turns, Returns, and Counter-turns were never match'd, nor are ever to be reached again.

(k) Ariſtoph. *equites.*   (l) Περὶ ἀφύων.

Who follow'd him in Comedy were content to trifle with the Punks, the Pandars, the Ruffian, the old Chuff, the *Davus* or Knave of the Family, and his young Master.

Amongst the Moderns, our *Rehearsal* is some resemblance of his *Frogs*: The *Vertuoso*'s Character, and *Ben Johnson*'s *Alchymist* give some shadow of his *Clouds*; but nowhere, peradventure wanders so much of his Spirit, as in the *French Rabelais*.

We may trust *Horace* for the sence of the *Latins*, at the time when they were best able to judge. Then they reckon'd, as the *Greeks* had done, that the *End of Poetry* was as well to be profitable, as to be pleasant.

-----*Simul & jucunda, & idonea dicere Vitæ.*

But what their practice, or how they improv'd the *drama*, we see not. They tell of an *Oedipus*, written by *Julius Cæsar*; an *Alcmæon*, by *Catullus*; a *Thyestes* by *Gracchus*; an *Adrastus*, and an *Aiax* by *Augustus Cæsar*; an *Astyonax*, by *Rutilius*; a *Medea* by *Mecænas*; a *Medea* by *Ovid*; with *Seneca*'s *Medea* too. The Names of these several Tragedies import, that these great men were content to translate from the *Greek*, no farther then had their ambition carried them. *Horace* says, indeed,

Non

Non minimum meruere decus vestigia Græca.
Ausi deserere, & Celebrare domestica facta.

We find the name of *Octavia* by *Mecænas*; and *Diomedes* Instances in the *Brutus*, the *Decius*, and the *Marcellus*, for *Fables* of the *Roman Garb*; but we know no farther of them, what success they had, nor how nobly they perform'd what they had so boldly undertaken, in writing alone, without a *Greek* Copy before 'em. It seems but a faint Commendation (the *Non minimum*) that *Horace* gives them.

The *Romans* were a rougher sort of People; and wonderful jealous were they of the *Grecian Arts*, or of any Commerce with a Politer Nation. Till *Numa Pompelius*, very little had they of either Religion or Poetry amongst them. Nor made he use of it farther, than for the *Hymns*, and *Anthems* at the Altars and Sacrifice: Secular *Poetry* had they none. And indeed at that time it was hardly safe for *Poetry* to stir from Sanctuary; for in the world, the rigid Fathers had given the *Poets* an ugly name, calling them *Grassatores*; which in Modern *Italian* may be rendred *Banditi*.

It was with much ado, and under an Usurpation by the *Decemvirat*, that they stooped to a correspondence with *Greece*, for

the

the commodity of their Laws; which were not till then imported; and from thence we hear of the Twelve Tables.

For the (m) *Stage-Plays*: It was a Plague that first introduced them. They try, by that strange Worship, to appease their Gods; and avert the Judgment so heavy on them. But their first *Secular Plays* were taught by *Livius Andronicus*, some 200 years after the Twelve Tables at *Rome*. He set up for some skill in this *Dramatick* way, *Translating* from the *Greek*.

Nor did *Plautus* that followed him attempt any farther, than to *Translate*: yet carried he the *Drama* beyond what any *Roman* since could pretend to. He *Translates* indeed, but with that spirit and mastery, one might take him for an Original; did we not always find the *Scene* at *Athens*; and all the pother is some little jilting story, or knavish pranck: Proposing only some trifling silly Mirth or Pastime.

He had not the courage to trace *Aristophanes*, He had not an *Heart of Hercules*, to combat Vice. Perhaps in his time, they had not yet learn'd to make their *Doctrine* profitable; for he commends one for a rarity.

Hujusmodi paucas poeta reperiunt Comædias
  Ubi boni Meliores fiant.

After all the goodly commendations and

(m) *Livy. l. 7.*   pretty

pretty things, by *Quintilian* (n) acknowledged due to *Plautus*, and *Terence*, frankly he concludes, *in Comædia maxime Claudicamus ——vix levem Consequimur umbram*; That *the* Roman *is infinitely short of the Greek Comedy, hardly comes up to the shadow of it.* Horace would fain with some colour, (o) make good the Comparison betwixt the *Romans* and the *Greeks*; on that Topick, to flatter *Augustus*. But *Virgil*, with no disadvantage to his Compliment, gave up the Cause.

Excudent alii ——
Tu regere imperio populos, Romane, memento,
Hæ tibi erunt Artes ——

Let them have all the praises due to their polite Learning: *To govern and to give Laws, be these thy Arts, O* Cæsar *!* this is thy glory without a Rival.

On other occasions *Horace* declares his mind freely enough.

Terence complains heavily that he could not keep his Audience together: One while they ran after the Gladiators, another time the Blockheads would be gaping at a Rope-Dancer.

—— Rumor venit datum iri gladiatores——
---neque spectari, neque cognosci potuerit,

(n) *l.* 6.   (o) *Epist.*

Ita

Ita populus, studio stupidus in funambulo,
Annimum occuparat ——

Here might be a juft Fable, true Characters, good Sence, and neat Expreffion. Here might be Nature and Morality in a delicate turn of Words: But where is the *Show*? where is the *Action*, that are the *Fac totum* to the Spectators?

Upon the whole; This dramatick Poetry was like a forreign Plant amongft them, the Climate not very kindly, and cultivated but indifferently; fo might put forth Leaves and Bloffoms, without yielding any Fruit of much importance.

Athens was the genuine Soyl for it, there it took, there it flourifhed, and ran up to overtop every thing fecular and facred: There had this Poetry the Honour, the Pomps, and the Dignity; their Regalia, and their Pontificalia.

But the *Romans*, moftly look'd no deeper than the Show. They took up with the outfide and Portico; their Genius dwelt in their eye; there they fed it, there indulg'd and pamper'd it immoderately: So that their *Theatres* and their *Amphitheatres* will always be remembred, tho their *Tragedy* and *Comedy* be only fhadow; or *Magni Nominis umbra.*

They reckon'd thefe matters of wit and fpeculation, not fo confiftent with the
fe-

severity of an active warlike people: something of their old *Saturn* lay heavy in their heads to the very last.

———— *Hodieque manent vestigia ruris,*
says *Horace.*

And he gives the Reason;

Serus enim Græcis admovit acumina Chartis:
Et post Punica bella quietus quærere cæpit,
Quid Sophocles, quid Thespis, & Aeschylus utile ferrent.

CHAP. III.
The CONTENTS.

The first Christians cry against Idols, Stage-Plays, Pagan Worship. Apostolical Constitutions. Greek and Latin *Fathers.* Tertullian's *Conceipt. Councils against* Heathen Learning. Greek-Wisdom. *St.* Hierom, *St.* Austin, *their Sin of* Heathen Books. *A Canon that no Bishop read an* Heathen Book. *Julians Project. The Christians countermine. A Christian* Homer, Pindar, *and* Euripides. *Stage-Plays particularly levell'd at. The same heat at this day in the* Spanish Jesuits. Pedro de Guzman *against Stage-Plays, and Bull-feasts. The Name of Poet a Bugbear at the Reformation. The Heresie charged on Sing-Songs, and Stage-Plays.* Marot's Psalms. *How in vogue at the* French Court. *Reasons against Stage-Plays.* Lactantius. *The same* 2000 *years ago by* Plato. *Tragedy,* Homer, Aeschylus. *Objections by* Aristophanes.

WHEN our first Christians had scuffled out their way from amongst the *Jews,* and turn'd their back on *Palestine,* they were put to a new sort of Game with the *Gentiles.*

The *Law* and the *Old-Testament-Prophets* stood 'em no longer in stead; they must now conjure up the *Sibyls*, and call the Philosophers to their assistance. And as *Idolatry* had been the most roaring sin amongst the *Isralites*; their main Cry still is against *Idols*; and nothing stood so full in their face as did the *Theatres*; where Tragedies and Commedies on the *Good Times* and *Festivals* were presented as the greatest and most solemn part of the *Pagan Worship*: For these had their Altars, and the particular Gods to which they were consecrated. (a) *Idolatriæ ab initio dicata, habent prophanationis suæ maculam.*

No wonder then if the *Theatre*, with all its Ministers and dependants, had a very ill name in the first Ages of Christianity. Hence it was, that if any body had to do with the (b) *Theatre*, the Apostolical Constitutions would not allow him *Baptism.* Saint *Cyril* afterwards declares, that when *In our Baptism we say, I renounce thee, Satan, and all thy works and Pomps: Those Pomps of the Devil are Stage-Plays, and the like vanities.* To the same Tune *Tertullian*, (c) That *in our Baptism renouncing the Devil and his Pomps, we cannot go to a Stage-Play without turning Apostates.*

(a) Tertull. *de Idol.* (b) *c.* 3. *l.* 8. (c) *L. de Spec.*

Hence

Hence indeed the *Greek* and *Latin* Fathers had an ample Field for their Eloquence and Declamation, before the *Arrians*, the *Gnosticks*, and other inteftine Herefies fprang up to divert them. So we find St. *Cyprian*, St. *Bafil*, *Clement* of *Alexandria*, very warm upon this occafion: And in many a good Homily St. *Chryfoftom* puts it home to 'em, and cries fhame, that people fhould liften to a Comedian with the fame ears that they hear an Evangelical Preacher.

St. *Auftin* (d) will have thofe that go to Plays, as bad as any that write, or act them; *Nullo modo potuiſſe Scriptiones & actiones recipi Comædiarum, niſi mores recipientium Conſonarent.* But *Tertullian* runs it off beyond all of 'em, with a notable Conceipt againft the Tragedians: (e) *The Devil*, fays he, *fets them upon their high Pantofles to give Chriſt the lie, who faid, no body can add one Cubit to his Stature. Tragædos Cothurnis extulit Diabolus, quia nemo poteſt adjicere Cubitum unum ad Staturam ſuam, & ſic Mendacem facere vult Chriſtum.*

Thefe Flafhes from fingle Authors, and drops of heat, had no fuch wonderful effect, but that the Tragedian ftill walk'd on in his high fhooes; yet might they well expect a more terrible ftorm from the Reverend Fathers, when met in a body together, in

(d) *Epiſt.* 202. *Nectar.* (e) *l. de Spect.*

Council *Oecumenical*. Then indeed began the Ecclesiastical Thunder to fly about, and presently the Theatres, Tragedy, Comedy, Bear-baiting, Gladiators, and Hereticks, are given all to the Devil, without distinction.

Nor was it sufficient for the zeal of those times to put down Plays. All Heathen Learning fell under the like censure and condemnation. One might as well have told them of the *Antipodes*, as perswaded the reading of *Tully*'s Offices: They were *afraid of the Greek Philosophy, like Children of a Bug-bear, least it fetch 'em away.* (f)

What a plunge was (g) St. *Hierom* put to, by *Rufinus*, laying to his charge the *reading of Heathen Authors*? How St. *Austin* heartily begs God (g) pardon, for having *read* Virgil *with delight*, in his greener years? (h) It was not only against the *Figmenta poetarum*, that their Canons levell'd: A Council of *Carthage* would not allow that *a Bishop should read any Heathen Book*. (h)

This blind Zeal gave a pleasant prospect to the *Apostate Julian*: And he might well foresee what this new Religion was like to come to, without a new set of Miracles to support it. He therefore was, in this, for complying with them, and seconded their Designs; making a Law, that no Christion should be taught

(f) *Clem. Strom.* (g) *In* Ruf. (h) *Conc.* 4. *Can.* 16.

in

n the Heathen Schools, or make use of that Learning. This made the Christians suspect a Snake in the Grass, and put them on the other hand,(a) upon a Counter-Plot, to frustrate his project. So *they set to work* Apollinarius, *a person, very luckily then ; of manifold Learning and Wit ; who, in the room of* Homer, *composed for them the History of the Old Testament in Heroick Verse, down to the Times of* Saul.

And Comedies also in imitation of Menander, *together with Trageaies, like those of* Euripides; *and* Lyricks, exactly *to the strain of* Pindar. An old Author, in his life of *Gregory Nazianzen*, assures us how that that holy Prelate undertook and performed the very same thing, *so defeated the purpose of that wicked Tyrant*. These Noble Labours have all dropt short of us ? What Philosophers, what Conjurers should we have been? how our Ears would ha' tingled at this day, with the three *Homers*, and a Triple Round of all the Græcian Poetry ? But the *Fathers* and *Councils* for several Ages declaring against every thing of *Heathen* denomination ; the *Stage-Plays*, of course, were cry'd out upon, as *Pagan Practice, Heathen Tradition, Rags and Relicks of Paganism, and Pagan Idolatry*, in

(a) *Sozomen Hist. Ecclef. l. 5. c. 17.*

D *vented*

vented by the Devil, and appropriated to the *Worship of false Gods.*

And, upon this Topick, to this day, we find the Spanish Jesuits wondrous Eloquent. Says *Pedro de Guzman* (*b*); *The Christian Emperours, Kings, and Popes have cut off, and burnt with the fire of their holy Zeal, many Heads of that old* Hydra *of Pagan Leudness : But yet there be two Heads that still remain, which cause a world of mischief : These two Heads also must be lopt off and burnt down to rights*; to wit, *y Comedias y los Juegos de Toros,* Comedies, and the Bull-Feasts.

At the beginning of the Reformation, the name of Poet was a mighty Scar-Crow to the *Mumpsimus* Doctors every where. The German Divines, and Professors at *Kullen*, were nettled and uneasie by this Poet, and the t'other Poet (*c*); Poet *Reuclin*, Poet *Erasmus*. Every body was reckoned a Poet that was more a Conjurer than themselves. And, belike, the *Jesuits* are still of Opinion, That the *Stage-Plays* have not done 'em service. *Campanella* tells us, that *the German and Gallican Heresie began with Sing-Song, and is carried on by* (*d*) *Comedy, and Tragedies. Ex Cantilenis incepit Hæresis Germanica & Gallicana, Comœdiis &*

(*b*) *Dis. 5. § 1.*   (*c*) *Epist. Obsc.*   (*d*) *l. Poetic. c. 6.*

Tragœdiis

Tragœdiis nutritur; Meaning, perhaps, *Marots* Translation of the *Psalms.* The *Sorbone* declared against them, yet were they so much in vogue at the French Court, that no person of Note, but had their favourite Psalm to their occasions. King *H.* 2. chose the 42 Psalm, *Ainsi qu' on oyt le Cerf. Like as the Hart doth------* which he sung when a-hunting. *Madam de Valentinois,* who was in Love, took the 130. *Du fond de ma pensée---From the bottom of my heart,* which she sung *en volte.* The Queens choice was the 6th, *Ne vueillez pas o Sire, Lord, in thy wrath ---* to an Air on the *Chant des buffons. Anthony* King of *Navarr* had the 43th, *Revange moy, prens ta querelle. Judge, and revenge my Cause* (e), which he tun'd to the *Brawl of Poictiers,* and the rest in like manner. *Clement Marot* set their Pipes a-going in Court and Countrey. And the poor Hereticks keep it up to this day; tho' (God-wot) they now (many of them) *sing their Song in a strange Land.*

To be call'd Apostate; to be deny'd our Baptism, Eucharist, and Christian Burial; to be Excommunicated, and given up to the Devil by so many Fathers, Canons, and Councils; however terrible to the Ears, is

(e) *Florimond Ramond, Hist. Hæres.*

not so convincing to the Understanding, as one fair Argument from Reason. What occurs of this kind is peradventure mostwhat comprehended in these words of *Lactantius.*

Comicæ Fabulæ de stupris Virginum loquuntur, aut amoribus Meretricum: Et quo (f) magis sunt eloquentes qui flagitia illa finxerunt, eo magis sententiarum elegantia persuadent. Et facilius inhærent Audientium memoriæ versus numerosi & ornati. Tragicæ Historiæ subjiciunt oculis Parricidia, & Incesta, & Cothurnata scelera demonstrant.

In Comedies, says he, *are represented the debauch, and leud Pranks amongst Women of evil Conversation: And the more excellent that the Poet is, the deeper is the impression on the hearers. The Neatness and Elegance of Thought, with the Beauty and Sweetness of the Verse, run always in their mind, and will not out of their head. Tragedy lays before 'em Parricides, Incests, and Wickedness in its Pontificalibus.*

This indeed is of weight, and deserves consideration. It is a standing Objection; and was a Pagan Objection above two thousand years ago.

Plato is very particular in his charge; says he, Fraud and Rapine, (g) and all

(f) *Lib. 6. Inst. Div.* (g) *l. Common. Dial. 2.*

manner

manner of violence they commend or countenance by good Presidents, and Examples of this, and t'other God, or Son of God. *Mercury* is made the Patron for stealing. And how scurvily does *Jupiter* deal with his Old Father? What piques, fewds and domestick squabbles amongst themselves? nor is their War with the Giants a more tolerable fiction. *(h)* Whatever is devised of this kind is a false fable, and a lye, and yet, were it true, not fit to be divulged to the people. *(i)* God is never to be represented whether in Songs, in Psalms, or Tragedy, otherwise than Just, Good, and Gracious. And on no account, to be said the author of Evil. When any evil is done the Cause is to be sought for elsewhere. Nor is it to be imagin'd that God had any hand in't. Therefore is it not to be endured that any Poet should as *Homer* (*k*), give out, that,

Two Barrels in his Cellar Jove *has still*
 Of gifts to be bestow'd on Mortal Wights,
One full of good, the other full of ill,
 And usually to mingle them delights.

Nor must be suffer'd that infraction and violation of the Oaths and Truce by (*l*) *Pan-*

(*b*) L. of Laws, Dial. 12. (*i*) *Commonw. ut supra.* (*k*) *Il. ω.* (*l*) *Il. Δ.*

darus

darus when done at the inftigation of *Jupiter* and *Minerva*.

Nor that broyl and controverfie amongſt the Gods, put to the Arbitration and Decifion of *Jupiter* and *Themis*.

Nor can *Æfchylus* be allow'd to ven any thing like that faying,

Whom Jove *wou'd deftroy he takes awa their Senfes.*

Nor, if in any fort of Poetry relation i made of the affliction that befel to *Niobe* or to the *Pelopidæ*, or to the *Trojans*; o the like: It muft not be fuggefted that thi was the work of God: but if it be; then reafon is to be fubjoyned, as that God dic indeed, what was good and juft, and di chaftife 'em, for their good. But he muſt not fay that punifhment is an Affliction, anɗ that God afflicted them. For that woulɗ neither be Pious, be Profitable, nor b Confiftent.

Nor muft he reprefent God difguifin himfelf and putting on feveral fhapes t carry on fome Cheat or Impofture, nor t be capable of any Change, Paffion, or Per turbation. Nor fay that the *Gods wande from Town to Town in the likenefs of Stran gers*(*m*). And fuch Lies as are abroad, of *Pro teus* and *Thetis*. And in fome Tragedies

(*m*) 'Οδυσ. γ.

Juno turned into a Prieſt, gathering the benevolence of the Congregation for the Sons of *Inachus*, newly reſtored to life.

Nor is the lying Dream, ſent by *Jupiter* to *Agamemnon* (*n*) by any means to be excuſed.

Nor *Æſchylus* where he brings in *Thetis* complaining that at her Wedding *Apollo* in her *Epithalamium* ſung:

That long the Son of Thetis *was to live;*
By no diſeaſe moleſted. That the Gods
Took of my Fortunes care and ſpecial liking;
And gave me joy, and praiſes in abundance.
Cou'd my hopes fail, thus founded on Apollo,
His Mouth Divine, Fatidical, and True?
Yet He, the ſame, that flatt'red me ſo fair,
And at my Table ſat a willing gueſt,
He, that thus did and ſaid, even He has ſlain
                                                (*my Child.*

And in *Homer*, when ſhe cries out (*o*),

Ah wretched Goddeſs that I was to bear
The beſt of all the Heroes---

And when *Jupiter* mourns ſo heavily (*p*):

Ah me! my Son Sarpedon *will be ſlain----*
And for the honour of his Son ſo dear,
For Rain he drops of blood from Heaven ſends.

(*n*) *Il.* 2. (*o*) *Il.* Σ. (*p*) *Il.* π.

And when he laughs at *Vulcan* limping along with a Cup of *Nectar*.

And then the Gods laught all at once out-right
To see the lame, and footy Vulcan *skink* (*q*).

Æschylus had, in *Athens*, made a great noise with his Tragedy call'd the *Furies*: after which *Aristophanes*, to expose the Tragick Poets wrote a Comedy, which he nam'd the *Frogs*: There he charges *Euripides* for having brought upon the Stage, *Phædra*'s, *Sthenobæa*'s, and the like wicked Strumpets. Nay.

What is he not guilty of?
Has he not shewn you panders,
And Women bringing forth in Temples?
And such as mix with their own Brothers?
And those that say: Not to live is to live?
Thus has he fill'd the Town
With Scribes, Buffoons, and Monkeys,
That banter, and make Asses of the People.

He again twits him with his,

Τις οἶδεν, εἰ τὸ ζῆν μέν ἐςι καθανεῖν,
τὸ πεῖν δέ δειπνεῖν, καὶ τὸ καθεύδειν κώδιον;

(*q*) *Il. a.*

Who can tell but that to live is to dye,
To drink is to think, and to sleep, a woolsack.

This second line is added to ridicule the former, and for this sentence he taxes *Euripides* as teaching *Scepticism*; And everywhere is playing upon that,
My Tongue did Swear, my Mind was never Sworn.
As if thereby *Euripides* opened a door to Equivocation and Perjury.

Thus we see how well *Aristophanes*, and *Plato* agree with *Lactantius*; and charge upon Tragedy the same enormities, Incests, and *Cothurnata scelera*, and also the odd unlucky sayings that stick in our memory, and will not out of a body's head.

When King *Archelaus* asked *Plato* what book he might read to learn the state of Affairs and Government in *Athens*, *Plato* bid him only to read *Aristophanes*; 'tis likely that we may better trust him for the *State of Poetry* in his time. And we may be confident he would mince nothing, out of any favour or affection, being a professed Enemy to *Euripides*.

Upon a presumption then that nothing more can be rais'd to bear against this sort of Poetry; we may proceed to offer something in answer to those objections. CHAP.

CHAP. IV.

Ariſtotle's *general Anſwer evaſive.* Plato *a better Divine. Not better than our Modern. God may uſe ill inſtruments. The falſe Dream. The two Barrels. Fables before* Homer. *He of God ſenſibly.* Plato, Cant. *Metaphore the utmoſt we are capable of. Fables. Allegory.* Celſus to Origen *againſt the Bible. Allegory, a cure for all.* Homers *Fables from the Bible. The falſe Dream, from the Story of* Achab *improv'd by* Homer. Averroes *of Arabian Poets.* Apollo Loxias. *Particular ſentences. Texts of Scripture.* Juno, Job's *Wife.* SS. *in Vulgar Tongue.* Euripides, *ill Women. No blame to the art. Pomp of the Theatre. What ill names by Jeſuits.*

FOR every Cavil, againſt any thing deviſed by the Poets, in relation to the Gods, (*) *Ariſtotle* propoſes one general anſwer, That a Critick need not be ſo fierce and poſitive to quarrel on that account, where all are in the dark, that nei-

(*) *Poetica.*

ther

ther Critick nor Poet know ought of the matter. We may grant that this anfwer is evafive; And may allow that *Ariftotle* might not be fo great a Divine as *Plato*: yet, doubtlefs our Modern Divines are a match for *Plato*: And have the better end of the Staff in this controverfie. Who all hold with *Homer* and the old Poets that God may to good ends and purpofes, make ufe of evil means, and inftruments.

And thus was *Pandarus* employ'd by *Jove* and *Pallas* to break the Peace. And the lying Dream fent to cheat *Agamemnon*.

---*A Dream he call'd, falfe Dream, faid he,*
Go, hye to Agamemnons *Tent, and fay,*
Diftinctly, as you bidden are by me.
Bid him bring up his Army now to Troy,
For now the time is come, he fhall it take.

Objections of this kind make no difficulty now-adays, with the moft Orthodox: nor do the *two Barrels in* Jove's *Cellar*, make any ill found: we know with what Heifer they have plowed; and fee the Original of all the Greek Mythology; their Gods, and Heroes.

Not to reprefent their Gods with face, and fingers, with actions, and paffions, and
other

other Modifications, after the fashions of men, were to say nothing. St. *Paul* that soared as high as any body, and had the gift of Tongues, declares the things above *ineffable*. *Homer* knew this; therefore would not *banter* the World with hard words, and unintelligible gibberish, as *Plato* and others have since done; but did accommodate his Speech to our Human Senses, by Metaphors, Similitudes, Tropes, and Parables; after the manner of *Moses*, and the Old Prophets before him. He entertains and fills us to the utmost of our Organs and Capacity. Something he finds for all our Senses. He brings them to our Eyes, our Ears, our Touch: *Nectar* he provides for our Taste, and there always exhales an Ambrosial Odour in the Divine Presence. What *Plato*, or an Angel would say further, passes all understanding, would not enter our Organs; could have no relish or proportion to affect us, more than the Musick of the Spheres. Metaphor must be the Language, when we travel in a Countrey beyond our Senses.

The wisest part of the World were always taken with *Fables*, as the most delightful means to convey Instruction, and leave the strongest Impression on our Mind.

Mind. They in the (a) *East* will not be perswaded that the *Fables*, with us, under the name of *Æsop*, were other than of their Countrey growth: And *Lockman* they avouch to be the Author of them.

The Old Prophets could devise nothing higher for the future *Messiah*, than that every thing he should say would be a *Parable*.

As for the *Fables* which in *Homer*, or on the Stage give offence: The Antients had a thing call'd an *Allegory*, which went a great way towards stopping the mouth of many a pert Observator.

We see the word in the Apostle St. *Paul*, (b) and the application of it, which St. *Origen* was glad to find, when *Celsus* call'd him to account for the *Old Testament*; so many odd *Tales*, Eve *with the Serpent*, Cain *and* Abel: *the building of* Babel, Sodom, *with* Lot *and his Daughters*, (c) *Parricidia, & Incesta, & Cothurnata scelera, far beyond any thing fabled in Tragedies of* Thyestes: Θυεϛείων κακῶν ἀνομώτερα. *Shall we Christians only*, says he, *be denied the benefit of this Allegory? May not we be allowed our Mystery, and Tropological meaning?*

So we see what *Lactantius* objected against *Homer*, and the Heathen *Tragedies*, is by

(a) *Huet on Romance.* (b) *Galat. c. 4.* (c) *Origen against Celsus, l. 4.*

the Heathens objected against our *Bible*, and Religion.

But we need not be so angry on either hand. Find but out the *Allegory*, and we are all to-rights again.

Besides, it is now no secret, that *Homer* had most of his *Fables* from some Hebrew Tradition or Original. (d) *Clement* of *Alexandria*, and *Eusebius* made the discovery long ago.

So the lying *Dream* (e) sent by *Jupiter* to *Agamemnon*, which *Plato* was so much offended at, is a Poetical Improvement from the Story of *Achab*. What pretty turn and dress he sets it off in, to bend and fashion it into one piece with his Song; and to accommodate it the better to our Ears in a more Philosophical Climate?

Averroes, after his Comment on the *Poetica*, allows that *Aristotles* Rules do not much concern the Arabian Poets; *What then*, says he, *shall we conclude that he wrote not Rules for the Arabians? God forbid!* Aristotle *wrote Nature; he wrote for all Human kind*.

But the *Arabian* Fancies always are on the gallop: They are not to march in rank and file, nor be subject to our *Européan* Discipline. *Homer* understood their

(d) Strom. Pr. Evang.   (e) Il. l. 2. Commen. Dia. 2.

Spirit,

Spirit, and could make the best on't: He knew how to manage the fiery *Arab*, and bring the wildest *Asiatick* to his hand.

Æschylus is not to be blamed, when he tells of *Apollo* singing at a Wedding, that much happiness should ensue thereupon; and the Child should live long. *Apollo* before then had the Epithete of *Loxias*, from his double meaning; to shew the Nature of Oracles. Be not out of patience, *Thetis*, thy Child shall live, his memory, his better part. *Homer* has ensur'd it for *Achilles*, to the end of the World.

If then the Fables heretofore employed for the *Drama*, are not so hastily to be censured; no body, I conceive, will stick with us for the particular sayings, as before mention'd to be objected by *Aristophanes*, *Plato*, and *Lactantius*.

For their good sayings, we have St. *Paul* citing a whole Verse out of a Comedy of *Menander*. St. *Clemens* of *Alexandria* brings more proofs for Christianity from *Menander* and other Comedies, than from all the Bible, or any other Topick.

On the other hand, where ill men are represented, we must not take it amiss that they say ill things. *Dolus an Virtus, quis in hoste requirit?* When we remember the saying, we remember it the saying of a

Rogue;

Rogue; of *Sinon*, as notorious amongst his Companions, as was *Judas* amongst the Apostles.

Flectere si nequeo superos, Acheronta movebo.

This by every body is allowed to be a very wicked saying. But why may not *Juno* sometimes take as much liberty of her Tongue, as *Job's Wife*, or any other Old-Testament Matron? There is no question but we find more abuse of the sayings in holy Scripture, and the consequence more Tragical, than from any perverted Text in Poetry. *Curse ye Meroz*, serves any bodies purpose, that would be cutting Throats. *Campanella* and *Pedro de Guzman* would urge as much against the S.S. in our Mother Tongue, on this account, as against this *Nurse of Heresie*, this *Hydra's Head* of Dramatick representations.

If there be any eye and inspection on the Pulpits, that they be kept to decency and Rule; May not the King and Queens Theatre deserve the like care, and have its Committee of Lay-Bishops to see that no Doctrine be there broached, but what tends to the Edification, as well as to the Delight of the Spectators.

If *Euripides* brought on the Stage Harlots

lots *(f)* *Æschylus* shew'd none; nor any Woman that might be so much as suspected to be in Love. What was an errour in one, is not to be charged on the rest; nor a Reflection on the Art. Indeed, when the Art is abused, one may with *Tully* cry out, *O præclaram Morum Emendatricem Poeticam!* But the same Irony is as applicable to the Pulpit, as to the Stage.

Grant there, in a Tragedy, the felicity of the Invention, the novelty of the Fictions, the strength of Verse, the easiness of Expression, the solid Reason, the warmth of Passion, still heightened and rising from Act to Act; together with the richness of Figures, the pomp of the Theatre, the habits, gesture and voice of the Actors, at the same instant charming both the Eyes and the Ears; so the Senses being won, the Judgment is surprised, and the whole Man at once led captive: A body must be of Brass or Stone to resist so many Charms, and be Master of himself amidst so much allurement and temptation.

Grant all this, I say, where is the hurt? what is the danger? If *the End* of all is to shew *Virtue in Triumph*. The noblest thoughts make the strongest impression; and the juster passions find the kindest re-

(a) Aristoph. Frogs.

ception amongſt us. The Medicine is not leſs wholeſom, for the Honey, or the gilded Pill. Nor can a Moral Leſſon be leſs profitable, when dreſſed and ſet off with all the advantage and decoration of the Theatre.

This is, indeed, of all diverſions the moſt bewitching; and the Theatre is a Magazine, not to be truſted, but under the ſpecial eye and direction of a Virtuous Government, otherwiſe, according to the courſe of the World, it might, poſſibly, degenerate; to deſerve the Aſperſions, and ill names, whereby the Jeſuits would render it odious, calling it the *School of Vice*, the *Sanctuary of Venus*, the *Temple of Impiety*, the *Furnace of Babylon*, the *Confiſtory of Impurity*, the *Shop of Leudneſs*, the *Peſt of Common-wealths*, the *Seminary of Debauchery*, *Satan's Feſtival*, and the *Devil's Dancing-School*.

CHAP.

CHAP. V.

Of Poetry in Italy. Ariſtotle's *Works.* Tramontains. *Cardinal* Bibiena. *Tragedy there with* Chorus. Strolers. Chriſt's Paſſion.

Of Poetry in France. Clem. Marot. Strolers *there. Proceedings at Law againſt them. Report of their Caſe. Their* Old Teſtament. Acts *of the* Apoſtles, *and* Chriſt's Paſſion. *Baniſh'd from* France. *Comedy there. Tragedy by* Hardy, Corneille, Richilieu. *Academy Royal. The Theatre. Caution that no* Equivoque, *nor ought againſt good Manners. More nice than the Pulpit. Their Gallantry,* Verſe, *Language, unfit for Tragedy. Dramatick repreſentations baniſh'd from* Spain. *Nurſe of Hereſie. Father* Guzman. Eſcobar.

Of Poetry in England. Britiſh, *Saxon, Norman, Latin and* Provencal *Poetry there.* Richard Ceur de Lion, *a* Provencial *Poet. Our Monks and Hiſtory falſe on that account. The Gay Science. That and the* Albigenſes *contemporany, and from the ſame Countrey. King* Richard's *Fellow-Poets.* Jeffry Rudel, *and Counteſs of* Tripoly.

IN the beginning of the laſt Century, when People began to open their Eyes, and look farther into the Matters of Religion and good Litterature, *Italy* had much the ſtart and advantage from the reſt of

Europe.

Europe, thither were *Aristotle*'s Works first brought a-shoar; and there were they translated, conn'd, and commented by the chiefest Wits amongst them. And above all, his *Poetica* engag'd their utmost care and application.

So many Comments had they made, and so many Critical Observations, before, on this side the *Alps*, any thing, in that way, was understood, that they began to lay it down for a truth, that the *Tramontans* had no *gusto*. Oltramontani, says one of them, *Non sono zelanti delle buone regole de Greci, & de Latini*. They make no Conscience of breaking the good Laws of the Greeks and Latins.

Others undertook to put in practice, and write by his Principles and Direction. *Bibiena* (afterwards a Cardinal) first try'd his Talent on a Comedy; and was followed by *Aciosto, Piccolomini, Machiavel*, and many others, who took *Plautus* and *Terence* for their Patterns.

Trissino, Ruscalli, Cinthio, Tasso, with many more, wrote Tregedies in blank Verse, with the *Chorus*, and every thing to the best of their power, after the Athenian Models.

But *Italy* had no *Fund* for the vast charge of Dramatick representations; they had no standing

(53)

standing Revenue for the Theatre; and however magnificent some Prince might be on an extraordinary Wedding or great occasion; there was nothing constant, nor could it, in such circumstances, be expected, that the *Drama* there should turn to account, or rise to any tolerable reputation. Therefore the ordinary business of the Stage was left amongst a company of *Strolers*, who wandred up and down, acting Farce, or turning into Farce, whatever they acted. * *Castelvetro* tells us, that even at *Rome*, in his time, *Christ's Passion* was so acted by them, as to set all the Audience a-laughing.

Francis the first, by whose Encouragement Letters had begun to flourish in *France*, and Poetry more particularly, by the means of *Clement Marot* (who then translated the *Psalms*, and sent abroad his *Balades*, which *Campanella* reckons to have ushered in the *Heresie*) King *Francis*, I say, was much delighted, for want of better, with these *Strolers*. At the latter end of his Reign we find a *Cause* of the *Strolers* notably pleaded and debated amongst their Lawyers and the King's Counsel.

The Charge against them extracted from the Parliament-Rolls, *Anno* 1541.

That They, 2 or 3 years ago, had under-

(*) Poetica.

taken

taken to represent Christ's Passion, *and the* Acts *of the* Apostles; *and therein had employed mean illiterate fellows, who were not cunning in those matters, as a Carpenter, a Bum-Bailiff, a Weaver, and others, who had committed divers faults, both in the* Fiction, *and in their* Action. *And to lengthen out the time, had interlarded many* Apocryphal *Matters, not contained in the* Acts *of the* Apostles, *that their Play might last three or four days longer; thereby to get the more Money from the People. Adding, moreover at the beginning, or at the end,* Drolls, *and wanton* Farces, *and by that means had made it hold out for six or seven months together: By means whereof the Divine Service was neglected, no body went to Church, Charity grew cold; besides all the Adulteries, Fornications, Mockeries, and Derisions unexpressible.*

More especially, in the first place, on Holy-days, from eight or nine a Clock a-mornings, the People left their Parish-Mass, Sermon, and Vespers, to take their place at the Play-house; and staid there till five in the Afternoon. So that Preaching was left off, the Preachers finding no body to hear them.

And the People, as they came back from the Play-house, would publickly and loudly mock at the Plays and Actors, repeating some words they had heard knockt out of joynt, at the Play;

or

or some part ill acted, saying in derision, The Holy Ghost was loth to come down, *and the like.*

And generally the Parsons of the Parishes to have their pastime at the Plays, have left off the Afternoon Prayers on Holy-days: Or have said them alone by themselves at Noon, an hour not usual, nor Canonical. And even the King's Chaplains, in the Chappel of the Houshold, whilst the Plays lasted, have on Holy-days said the Evening-Prayers at Noon: And besides, ran them off post-haste, to be gone to the Play-house: A thing undecent, unusual, of evil example, and contrary to the holy Councils of the Church, namely, the Council of Carthage, *where it is said,* Qui die solemni prætermisso Ecclesiæ conventu ad spectacula vadit, excommunicetur.

2. *Preaching is more decent for the Instruction of the People (provided 'tis done by Theologians, men of Learning and Knowledge) than are the Plays, made by those that are ignorant and illiterate; who neither know what they speak nor what they act; representing the* Acts *of the Apostles, the* Old Testament, *and the like Histories which they pretend to act.*

3. *It is plain by Natural Reason, that without first knowing the Truth, one cannot make a Fiction; for Fiction is to be something as near the Truth as may be; whereas neither*

E 4 *the*

the Masters, nor the Actors know the A B C. *They understand neither the Bible, nor any prophane Learning, being Mechanicks, as Coblers, Botchers, Porters, that can neither read nor write. nor have been train'd to the Stage, or that sort of exercise: Neither is their Tongue well hung, nor have they proper Language, nor can they accent the words, or give them a decent pronunciation: Nor do they know at all what they are about, or what it is they say; so that sometimes they chop one word into three, stop in the middle of a sentence, making it a question, which is a sentence of Admiration; accenting and pronouncing with their gesture every thing* Kim Kam, *quite contrary; causing a laughter, and hooting in the Play-house, that instead of turning to Edification, there is nothing but scandal and derision.*

4. *The Farces and wanton Interludes which they mix with the Mysteries Ecclesiastical, make it a thing forbidden by all the Councils, as the Doctors all agree.*

5. *It is visible that what they do is for Lucre only; as they would do with a Tavern, or Trade: And they raise the price, which the first year was twenty and twenty five Crowns, the next thirty and thirty six Crowns, and in this present year forty and fifty Crowns of the Sun, for every Box.*

6. *Great*

6. Great mischief, by Assignations, under colour of going to the Plays, Adulteries, &c.

7. The Plays occasion Junketing and expences extraordinary, amongst the common people; so that which a Handy-crafty-man has earn'd in a week, shall be all spent in one day, at the Plays, and the Junketing and Drunkenness, whereby his Wife and poor Children suffer all the week.

8. Charity so much impaired, that within the six weeks that the Plays have continued, the Alms are lessen'd 3000 Livres.

Nothwithstanding all which, one Royer, a Fish-seller, a Carpenter, a Cobler, and others their Companions have a-new for this next year undertaken to have acted the Old Testament, and set a price for hereafter to get money from the people.

Of all which, the King's Attorney General being informed, hath put a stop to their farther proceedings. They shew a Letter of Priviledge they had obtained from the King.

By the Letters it appears, they had suggested to the King, that what they did was out of pure Zeal and Devotion, and for the Edification of the People, which is false; and besides, their quality and circumstances speak the contrary; and what they do is barely a Trade for gain. Moreover, in the Old Testament are many things not so proper to be declared to the

People,

(58)

People, weak and simple, that may be drawn in to turn Jews *for want of understanding.*

For these considerations a stop is put to their Acting of the Old Testament, *till the good pleasure, will and intention of the King, when inform'd of those matters, shall be known.*

The said Attorney General also presented another Complaint against the former Company, that they might put into the Poors Box, out of their Profits, for their representing the Acts of the Apostles, *eight hundred Livres till farther order; the like against the Company that acted* Chri t's Passion.

The Council for the Strolers *saith, He comes not to answer the Charge against them that show the* Acts of the Apostles; *but for the new Company only of the Mystery, for the* Old Testament. *And true it is, that the King two years since having sometimes seen them Act the Mystery of* the Passion; *and by the account then made him, how well they played the* Acts of the Apostles; *and that it was worth his while also to see the Representation of the* Old Testament, - Royer *above-named, being then present, did promise the King to get the* Old Testament *Acted. And thereupon the King gave leave to the said* Ro er, *to have the Representation of the* Old Testament; *and granted him Letters Patents accordingly.*

This

This Record, abridg'd here, in the translation, giving so particular an History of the Stage in those days, is added at length in the Original, at the end of the Book.

King *Francis* liv'd about five or six years after. And then were the Comedians both *French* and *Italians*, all packt off, and banished the Kingdom.

In 1597. *Peter l' Ariveu* published Comedies, written, as he tells us, in imitation of the Antient Greeks, *Latins*, and Modern *Italians*. And the end he proposed was according to *Horace*,

Quelque profit, & contentement ensemble.

After him *Alexander Hardy* attempted Tragedy, whose works were published *ann.* 1625. Not long after succeeded the famous *Corneille*, who began to write for the Stage, after *Hardy*'s Model.

And now, if the *French* Theatre did not rise to equal the glory of the *Romans*, and Antient *Greeks*, it was not for want of Encouragement from the Government. Cardinal *Richelieu*, who had the power in his hand, did heartily and generously perform his part. He founded the *Academy Royal*, and more especially provided for the Theatre.

Yet

Yet with this Caution, (*a*) never to reprefent *Aucunes actions Malhonneftes, ny d'ufer d'aucunes paroles lafcives, ny a double entente, qui puiffent bleffer l' honnefteté publique.* And we find the Poets ftand corrected, and do pennance if they chance to offend againft this declaration. The liberty *de l' equivoque,* nor any *idée vilaine* will there efcape cenfure, even by the Audience. So the *Theodore* by *Corneille,* wou'd not take. No other reafon could be devifed by the Author, but the meer conceipt of her Proftitution, which was odious to the imagination. And He rightly obferves from thence, that our Theatres are much more delicate on thofe occafions, than were the Antient Fathers, or the Pulpits. Says he; *However 'tis fome fatisfaction to me that I fee the better and more found part of my Judges impute this ill fuccefs to that imagination of a Proftitution, which one could not endure; tho' 'twas well known, it would not take effect : And that to allay the horror of it, I made ufe of all the helps that art and experience could furnifh me withall. Amidft this difgrace, I rejoice to fee the purity of our Stage, to find that an hiftory, the faireft Ornament of the fecond book of St.* Ambros's *Virgins, appears too licentious to pafs on our*

(*a*) Lom. 13. Decl. 1641.

Stage,

Stage. What might have been said, if, like that great Doctor of the Church, I had shown the Virgin *in that infamous place, if I had described the various agitations of her mind, whilst she was in the place, if I had drawn the troubles she felt that instant she saw (her lover)* Didymus *come in to her; 'tis on this occasion that this great* Saint *makes Triumph that Eloquence which Converted St.* Austin, *it is for this spectacle, that He particularly invites the* Virgins *to open their eyes.*

I kept her from the sight, And so much as I could, from the imagination of my Audience. Yet after all my industry, the modesty of our Theatre is such, to dislike that little, which the necessity of my subject, forced me to make known.

In points of decency the French are certainly very delicate, and commendable. The noble encouragement they met withal, and their singular application have carried them very far in the improvement of the *Drama*. Nor were the Audience to be taxed for the hasty applause, they have often given to Plays of no great merit. It has been so in all Nations.

As, in Pictures, A man who had never seen such a thing before, wou'd find his amusement, and be in admiration at every Sign-post, or *Saracens head* that he Travels by by. The first Plays of *Corneille* were better, that is, more regular, than any before him, the Audience had never seen the like. Judgment runs, most-what by comparison: by Purple we Judge of Purple.

They now see the difference betwixt his first Essays, and the Plays composed in his riper years.

After all it is observ'd how much, that Wild-goose-chase of Romance runs still in their head, some Scenes of Love must every-where be shuffled in, tho' never so unseasonable.

The Grecians were for Love and Musick as mad as any Monsieur of 'em all; yet their Musick kept within bounds; attempted no Metamorphosis to turn the *Drama* to an *Opera*. Nor did their Love come whining on the Stage to Effeminate the Majesty of their Tragedy. It was not any love for *Briseis* that made *Achilles* so wroth; it was the affront, in taking his booty from him, in the face of the Confederate Army. This, his Stomach cou'd not digest.

---- nec gravem
Peleidæ stomachum cedere Nescij. Hor.

One, with the Genius of *Miguel Cervante*, might, doubtless, find matter for as good a Sa-a Satyr, from the French Gallantry, as He had done from the Spanish Chivalry.

Another objection, is their writing Plays in Ryme.

The *Hexameter* wou'd not pass in Greek or Latin Tragedy, for the language is to be *Agissante*, active. They reckon'd the *Jambick* to be the verse for business.

-- *Natum rebus agendis.* Hor.

The French seem the remotest in the World from this sort of Turn. Our Ear shou'd not be hankering after the Ryme, when the business should wholly take us up, and fill our Head. The words must be all free, independant, and disengag'd, no entanglement of Ryme to be in our way. We must clear the Decks, and down with the Ornaments and Trappings in the day of Action, and Engagement.

But they are not only fetter'd with Ryme, but their verse is the long *Alexandrin*, of twelve syllables: with a stop, or pause always in the middle.

As if a Latin Tragedy were written all in *Pentameters*. To the Tune of,

Hei mihi quod domino, non licet ire tuo;

Or,

Or, with us, to the Air of *Hopkins* and *Sternold*.

O sing unto the Lord, a new and joyful song.

A Man shou'd not trust his own Ear to Judge a forreign language by, but their own best authors are sensible of this halt in their verse, and complain of that *Cesure* and perpetual *Monotomy*, as they call it.

In fine their language it self wants strength and sinews, is too feeble for the Weight and Majesty of Tragedy. We see their Consonants spread on Paper, but they stick in the Hedge; they pass not their Teeth in their Pronunciation.

From *Spain* little observable can be expected in relation to Dramatick Poetry; Since *Campanella* had assur'd them that it is *the Nurse of Heresie*.

So Father *Guzman* informs us that his Catholick Majesty, *Phil.* II. (*b*) towards the end of his life, (when his Wisdom was *en su punto*, on the prick of perfection, old age being *la salsa de la sabiduria*, seeing neither *medio*, *o remedio* to reform them) did quite banish them the Country.

Then another Jesuit lets us to know how religiously the truly Catholick, *Phil.* IV.

(*b*) *Disc.* 6. 1. 8.

this very year 1646. hath packt them away as the common Plague from out the Kingdoms of *Spain*, by his Royal Edict.

Quam pie Phil, *IV. vere Catholicus Comœdias ab Hispaniæ regnis, hoc Anno* 1646. *ut Communem pestem regio ablegarit Edicto*, *Escobar. Mor. Theol.* So we see this *Nurse of Heresie*, this *Head of the Pagan Hydra*, is like to have no footing within the Catholick Majesties Dominions. The *Inquisition* and the *Muses* must not set their Horses together.

Since the decay of the Roman Empire this Island, peradventure has been more fortunate in matters of Poetry, than any of our Neighbours. Notwithstanding the present flourish and ostentation of the French Theatre: Our Wit might have made us the better Poets: tho' our honesty make us worse *Politicians*. We find of the *British* Poetry to this day. One of our oldest Medals bears an Harp on the Reverse, with the Name *Kunobeline* around it.

The Germans have often printed with *Plautus* a Comedy call'd *Querolus*; which no body now questions, but that it was written by *Gildas*, who lived *Anno.* 493.

After him *Thaliessin*, and *Merlin*, and others, had they not written in *Welch*, might yet deserve an esteem amongst us.

F   Our

Our *Saxon* Kings have their Grants, and Charters in *Ryme*, yet upon Record.

The first *William* came, singing *Roland*, to fight that decisive Battel, which wan him England. *Rolandi cantu inchoato, ut bellatorum animos accenderet, prælium Commiserunt.* As *Mat. Paris*, *Mat. Westminster*, *Will. Malmsbury*, *Knighton*, and the rest inform us.

And indeed, to write in *Latin* the World had not the like to our Poets of that Century *Joseph of Exeter*, wrote so much above the Age, that he was well-nigh lost from us; his Poem of the *Trojan War*, going a long time currant in Print for a *Classick*, under the name of *Cornelius Nepos*. He brings us to *King R*. I. with whom, and with *Baldwyn* Archbishop of *Canterbury*, He went to the *Holy War*.

This King, *Richard Cœur de lion*, and his Brother *Jeffrey* had formerly liv'd much in the Courts of several Princes, in and about *Provence*, so came to take delight in their Language, their Poetry (then call'd the *Gay Science*) and their Poets; which began not long before his time, to be in great vogue in the World.

The Italian (*c*) Authors acknowledge that the best part of their Language, and

(*c*) *Bembo. Speron Sperone*, &c.

of their Poetry is drawn from that of *Provence*, as, indeed, is also that of the Spinish, and other Modern Languages. It is certain that *Petrarch* (the Poet that the Italians brag most on to this day) wou'd show very empty, If the *Provencial* Poets had from him, all their own again. And, in truth, all our *Modern* Poetry comes from them.

Never was known that application, both in the Princes and People, as at that time every where to the *Provencial* Poetry, which gave one of (*d*) their Romancers the fancy that *Charlemain* made a *Donation* of *Provence*, to be the *Poets Patrimony*.

I should not be so large on this occasion but to antidote against an impression, our *Monks* of that time might otherwise make upon us. As, amongst the rest, *Roger Hoveden* tells, that this King *Richard, to raise himself a name*, went *about begging and buying verses and flattering* Rymes; *And by rewards enticed over from* France Singers *and* Jesters, *to sing of him in the* Streets. *And it was every where given out, that there was not the like of him, in the World again.* Hic ad augmentum & famam sui Nominis, emendicata carmina, & rithmos adulatorios comparabat, & de regno

(*d*) *Phil: de Mousks.*

Francorum

Francorum Cantores & Joculatores *allexerat ut de illo canerent in Plateis, & dicebatur ubique quod non erat talis in orbe.*

That these *Songsters* and *Jesters* were brought from *France* is most false. *France* had no pretentions thereabouts in those days. Those Countreys were *Fiefs* of the Empire. *Frederick* I. had *Enfeoffed Ramond Berenger* of the County of *Provence, Forcalquiers*, and places adjacent, as not long after *Frederick* II. install'd *William au courb nez*, Prince of *Orange*, King of *Arles* and *Viennes*: which family had formerly possess'd *Provence*. As truly, he might have said, they were brought from *Spain*: for *Ildefonso* King of *Arragon*, Count of *Provence, Barcelona*, &c. had given and settled on his Son this County of *Provence*. It may be noted that about the same time that the *Provencial* Poetry did flourish, did also spring up that *Heresy* of the *Albigenses* that so much alarm'd the Popish World, and cost so many *Crusades* to suppress them. *Ramond* Count of *Tholouse* was the Protector of the *Albigenses*, and was also a principal *Patron* of these Poets. *Guilhem* of *Agoult*, *Albert* of *Sisteron*, *Rambald* of *Orange* (names now reviv'd by the Duke of *Savoy*) and the like, were *Provencial* Poets; All the Princes that were in league

league together to support the *Albigenses* against *France* and the Pope, did encourage and patronize these Poets, amongst the rest a King of *Arragon* lost his life in the quarrel, at a Battel where *Simon Monfort* did command as chief of the *Crusade*.

From hence we may gather why the Monks were so angry at these *Singers* and *Jesters*. And did not like that the King should be so familiar with them.

One of them with King *Richard* was *Anselm Faydet*, of whom *Petrarch*.

---- Anselmo
& mille altri ne vidi: a cui la lingua
Lancia & spada fu sempre, & scudo & elmo

I saw, with many others, Anselm *there,*
Whose tongue was shield and helmet, sword
(and spear.

This *Anselm* was wont to write *Comedies*, and *Tragedies*; which in his own Country he could sell for 2 or 3000 *livres Turnois*; and some for more: And had several acted at his own charge. After King *Richards* death, he married a Nun, a Dame of quality, out of a Nunnery at *Aix*. And after went to live with the Marquess of *Monferrat*, who took part with the *Count* of *Tholouse*: And to him *Anselm* ventur'd to show

show a *Comedy*; which till then he had kept secret from every body: and there had it acted.

In one of his Poems he describes the Palace of *Love*, his Court, his State, his Power, which *Petrarch* chang'd, and fashion'd to his mind; and calls it, in his Book, *il triumfo di amore.*

Another of these *Jesters* was *Fouchet* of *Marseilles*, who upon the death of King *Richard*, went home, turn'd Monk, and rose to be Archbishop of *Tholouse*. *Dante* has him in his Paradise, and *Petrarch* of him thus

Folchetto: ch'a Marsilia il nome ha date,
& a Genova tolto: & al' estremo
Cangio, per miglior patria, habito & stato,

Another of these (with *Jeffrey* King *Richard*'s Brother) was *Jeffrey Rudel*, of whom *Petrarch*,

Gianfre Rudel, ch' uso la vela e'l remo
A cercar la sua morte---

Whilst this Poet was with our Prince *Jeffrey*, he was told, by Pilgrims that came from the *Holy Land*, so many fine things of the *Countess* of *Tripoly*, that he could stay no longer. He

He puts on a Pilgrims Weeds, takes a Voyage to *Tripoly*, fell sick by the way, and ere he came a-shore was almost dead. The *Countess* inform'd of this *Errantry*, went to the Ship, took him by the hand. He opened his Eyes, said, *Having seen her, he was satisfied*; so departed this life.

She made for him a most splendid Funeral, provided him a Tomb of Porphyry, and his Epitaph in Arabick Verse: And had his Sonnets all curiously copied over, and illumin'd, with Letters of Gold; was taken with Melancholy, and turned Nun: One of the *Songs* made in his Voyage, was this:

Trat, & dolent m'en partray
  s'yeu non vey est' amour de luench.
  e non say qu' ouras la veyray,
  car son trop nostras terras luench.
Dieu que fes tout quant veu, e vay:
  e form' á quest' amour de luench,
  my don poder al cor, car hay
  esper vezer l' amour de luench.
Segnour, tenes my per veray,
  l' amour qu' ay vers ella de luench.
  car per un ben que m'en eschai
  ha mille mals tant soy de luench.
Ja d'autre amour non janziray
  s'yeu nen jau dest' amour de luench.

q'una plus bella non en sa
en luec que sia, ny pres, ny luench.

Sad and heavy should I part,
  but for this Love so far away;
  not knowing what my ways may thwart,
  my Native Land so far away.
Thou that of all things Maker art,
  and form'st this Love so far away;
  give body's strength, then shan't I start,
  from seeing her so far away.
How true a Love to pure desert,
  my Love to her so far away!
  eas'd once, a thousand times I smart,
  whilst, ah! she is so far away.
None other Love, none other Dart
  I feel, but hers so far away,
  but fairer never touch'd an heart,
  than hers that is so far away

CHAP.

(73)

CHAP. VII.

Savery de Mauleon *a Provencial Poet. Testimony of him.* King R. I. *His Verses when Prisoner in* Austria. *The Emperor* Frederick Barbarossa. *His Poetry.* Ramond Beringhier. *Four Daughters, four Queens.* Rob. Grosthead. *His Provencial Poetry. Other Languages stubborn.* Chaucer *refin'd our English. Which in perfection by* Waller. *His Poem on the Navy Royal, beyond all Modern Poetry in any Language. Before him our Poets better expressed their thoughts in Latin. Whence* Hoveden *might mistake, and his Malice. A Translation from* Grosthead. *The Harp a Musick then in fashion. Five Tragedies from* Joan *Queen of* Naples. *Forreigners all call'd French. Plays by the Parish-Clerks of* London. *What under* H. VIII. *flourish under Queen* Elizabeth. *The* Gorboduck. *French much behind-hand with us. Tragedy, with us, but a shadow.*

Savery *de Mauleon,* mentioned in our English Histories, is reckoned another of these *Provencial* Poets; of him an old * Bard, amongst them, gave this Testimony:

*Doussament fait motz & sos
ab amor que' m' a vencut.*

(*) *Guilhem Briton, MSS. with Signior Redi.*

Sweetly

*Sweetly could he say and sing
of Love, that me hath vanquished.*

And the same Author says of King *Richard*,

*Coblas a teira faire adroitement
pou vos oillez enten dompna gentilz.*

*Stanza's he trimly could invent,
upon the Eyes of Lady gent.*

One *Stanza*, of a Song made by him, when a Prisoner in *Austria*, may serve for a taste.

*Or sachan ben mos homs, e mos Barons,
Anglez, Normans, Peytavins, e Gascons;
qu'yeu nou ay ja si paure Compagnon,
que per aver lou laissess' en preson.*

*Know ye, my Men, my Barons all,
In England, and in Normandy,
In Poicters, and in Gascony,
I no Companion held so small,
To let him thus in durance lie.*

Our King *Richard* had not the Expedient of the French King St. *Lewis*, who, taken Prisoner by the Sarazens, pawn'd the Eucharist, body

body for body, to the Infidels for his Ransom.

Signior *Redi*, now with the great Duke of *Tuscany*, tells us the Mss. with King *Richard's* Poetry (*), and many other of the Provencial Poets are in his keeping.

This of the Emperor *Frederick I.* is currant every where.

> *Plas my Cavallier Francez,*
> *e la donna Catallana,*
> *e l' ourar Gynoez,*
> *e la Cour de Kaſtellana,*
> *lou Kantar Provenſales,*
> *e la danſa Trivyzana,*
> *e la corps Arrogonez*
> *e la perla Julliana,*
> *les mans e Kara d'Angles,*
> *e lou donzel de Thuſcana.*

I like in France *the Chivalry,*
The Catalonian Laſs for me,
The Genoes for working well,
But for a Court commend Caſtile.
For Song, no Countrey to Provance,
And Treves *muſt carry't for a dance.*
The fineſt ſhapes in Arragon,
In Juliers *they ſpeak in Tune.*
The Engliſh for an hand and face,
For Boys, troth, Tuſcany's *the place.*

(*) *Redi Dithyrambick.*

They

They who have written the lives of the Provencial Poets, with King *Richard*, and the Emperor *Frederick Barbaroſſa*, give us alſo the life of *Ramond* Count of *Provence*, memorable for his four Daughters, married to ſo many Kings. *Margaret*, to *Lewis* King of *France*. *Elionor* to our *H.* III. *Sance*, to *Richard* King of the Romans, *Beatrice* to *Charles* King of *Naples* and *Sicily*. On this occaſion, thus *Dante*.

Quattro figlie hebbe, & Ciaſcuna reina
Ramondo Beringhieri.---

Four lovely Daughters, each of them a Queen,
Had Ramond Beringher.---

Neither were the Churchmen all of the ſame Kidney with the Monks: as may be gather'd from the famous Biſhop of *Lincoln Rob. Groſthead*; the moſt eminent in his time for Piety and Learning, and the Man of greateſt Authority, who when living made the old Gentleman in St. *Peters* Chair tremble, and the bare Ghoſt of him, afterwards ſo thumpt off the Pope, that he died of the contuſion. He compos'd ſeveral treatiſes in this Provencial Ryme and Language. One of them, in *Bodleys* Library, bears this title:

Tractatus

Tractatus in lingua Romana secundum Dom. Rob. Grosstefte Lincoln Ep. de Principio Creationis Mundi.

The beginning is this:

Ki pense ben, ben peut dire :
Sanz penser ne poet soffire
De nul bon oure Comencer
Deu nos doint de li penser
De ki, par ki, en ki font
Toz les bens ki font el mond.

He that thinks well, well can say.
Without thinking, nought he may :
Not a good work once begin.
God wou'd have us think of him :
From whom, by whom, in whom are all
The good things which the World we call.

This *Provencial* was the first, of the modern languages, that yielded and chim'd in with the musick and sweetness of ryme; which making its way by *Savoy* to *Monferat*; The *Italians* thence began to file their *volgare*; And to set their verses all after the Chimes of *Provence*. Our Intermarriages, and our Dominions thereabouts, brought us much sooner acquainted with
their

their Tongue and Poetry? And they, with us, that would write verse, as King *Richard, Savery de Mauleon,* and *Rob. Grostead,* finding the English stubborn and unweildy, fell readily to that of *Provence,* as more glib, and lighter on the Tongue. But they who attempted verse in English, down till *Chaucers* time, made an heavy pudder, and are always miserably put to't for a word to clink: which commonly fall so awkard, and unexpectedly as dropping from the Clouds by some Machine or Miracle.

Chaucer found an Herculean labour on his Hands; And did perform to Admiration. He seizes all Provencal, French or Latin that came in his way, gives them a new garb and livery, and mingles them amongst our English: turns out English, gowty, or superannuated, to place in their room the foreigners, fit for service, train'd and accustomed to Poetical Discipline.

But tho' the Italian reformation was begun and finished well nigh at the same time by *Boccace, Dante,* and *Petrarch.* Our language retain'd something of the churl; something of the Stiff and Gothish did stick upon it, till long after *Chaucer.*

Chaucer threw in Latin, French, Provencial, and other Languages, like new Stum

to

to raise a Fermentation; In Queen *Elizabeth*'s time it grew fine, but came not to an Head and Spirit, did not shine and sparkle till Mr. *Waller* let it a running. And one may observe by his Poem on the Navy, *An.* 1632, that Not the language only, but His Poetry then distinguish'd him from all his contemporaries, both in *England* and in other Nations; And from all before him upwards to *Horace* and *Virgil*. For there, besides the Language Clean and Majestick, the Thoughts new, and noble; the Verse sweet, smooth, full and strong; the turn of the Poem is happy to Admiration. The first line, with all that follow in order, leads to the conclusion, all bring to the same point and centre,

To his own chosen more indulgent, He
Dares trust such power with so much piety.

Here is both *Homer* and *Virgil*; the *fortis Achilles*, and the *pius Æneas*, in the person he Compliments, and the greatness is owing to his Vertue. The Thought and Application is most Natural, Just, and true in Poetry, tho' in fact, and really, He might have no more fortitude or piety, than another body. For the repairing then of *Pauls* gave a reasonable colour for his Piety; And
that

that Navy Royal might well give him the pre-eminence in power, above *Achilles*. whoever before that time, tryed the same thoughts in Latin and in English verse; the former always had the advantage; the expression being more lively, free, elegant, and easie: Whereas in the English some thing or other was still amiss; force or affectation, poverty or superfluity mangling or disguising, pinching or encombring it.

Amongst the names for these *Provencial* Poets in their own Countrey, they were call'd *Troubadours*, *Jeongleors*, and *Chanterres*, the last word is not forreign to our Cathedrals, the second *Roger Hoveden* render'd *Joculatores*, as we may turn the first to Trompeters, but the *Troubadours*, or *Troverres* were so named from their Invention, as we say *tresor troue*, and the Italians call them *Trovatore*; And *Jongleors* was given them from some Musical instrument then in use, as the Greek or Latin, that were call'd *Lyrick* Poets. So our *Rob.* of *Grosthead* might then be a *Jongleor*, from his delight in the Harp, as we find in a preface to one of his Books in *Bodleys* Library, part of which is this.

For lewed men y undyrtoke,
In Englysh Tonge to make this Boke;

For

For many beyn of feeche manere
That Talys and Rymys wyle blethly here,

In Gamys and Festys and at the ale
Love men to lestene trotonale.

To alle Cryftyn men under Sunne
And to gode men of Brunne,

And specially alle by name
The felawshepe of Sympzynghame
Robert of Brunne gretyth zow.

The Zers of Grace fyl than to be
A thousand and three hundred and three

Yn that tyme turned ey thys
In English Tonge out of Frankys.

I shall zow telle as y have herd
Of the bysschop Seynt Robert

Hys name ys Grostefte
Of Lyncolne so seyth the geste

He lovede moche to here the Harp ――

The Harp, it seems, was in reputation at that time; And in *Provence* might be no hindrance to their matters of Piety; nor be ill Musick for the *Albigenses*, and the

Heresie of Lions. They had their Godly Romances, their *Turneament* of *Antichrist*, and *Fantamarie del Paganesmo*, and the like. Some wrote the Wars and Prowess of several Kings and Princes, the King of *Arles* against the Saracens, *la guerra delli Baulsensi*, the War of the Princes of *Baulx* (the Prince of *Orange*'s Family, &c.) but Comedy and Tragedy was what most of them offer'd at in their way.

The famous *Joan*, Queen of *Naples*, gave subject, to one of the last of those Poets, for five Tragedies: call'd by him, 1. The *Andreassa*. 2. The *Taranta*. 3. The *Maiorichina*. 4. The *Alemanna*, from *Andreas*, from a Prince of *Taranto*, a Prince of *Maiorca*, a German Prince (of the House of *Brunswich*) her four Husbands, murder'd by her. 5. *Giovannella*, from her own just and ignominious catastrophe.

By all this History we see the assertion of *Campanella* was not without foundation. And for the same cause our Monks might well be jealous of King *Richard*, and dislike in our other Kings, about that time, their great Correspondence and Alliances in *Provence*.

So the great cry in *Henry* the III. time (who with his Brother *Richard*, had Married

ried two of the Daughters of that Count of *Provence*, was againſt the *French:* (by that name noting all Forreigners.---)

**To remue þe Frenſſe men to libbe beyond ſe,
Bi hor londs her and ther, and ne come noght age.

And to granti God laws and þe old Charter alſo,
Þat ſo ofte was igranted er, and ſo ofte undo.*

And yet from this Marriage, ſprang thoſe our Kings which afterwards conquered *France.*

Theſe reflections have drawn me too far beyond my purpoſe, which was only to treat of dramatick repreſentations. (*e*) Of which kind *Stow* tells us that in the time of *R*. II. *An.* 1391. the *Pariſh Clerks* of *London* Acted a Play at the Skinners Well by *Smithfield*, which laſted three days ; and was of Matters from *Adam* and *Eve*. And in *H*. IV. his time, *Ann.* 1409. another was repreſented at the ſame place, which held eight days.

From this, and what was noted before in *France* and *Italy*, we may gather that the *Old Teſtament*, *Chriſts Paſſion*, and the *Acts of the Apoſtles*, were the ordinary en-

* *Rob. Gloc.* Mss. *Cotton.* (*e*) Survey of *London.*

tertainment on the Stage, all *Europe* over, for an hundred year or two, of our greatest ignorance and darkness. But that in *England* we had been used to another sort of Plays in the beginning of *H*. VIII. Reign may be seen from that of the * *Laureat* on Cardinal *Woolsey*:

> Like Mahound in a Play;
> No man dare him withsay.

And in the same reign we find printed the Interludes of *John Heywood*. But early under Queen *Elizabeth*, our dramatick Poetry grew to something of a just symmetry and proportion in 1566. *Geo. Gascoigne* of *Grays-Inn* translated the *Supposes*, from *Ariosto*, which was there acted: as also his *Jocasta* Englished from *Euripides*, the Epilogue witten by *Chr. Yelverton*.

And after that were reckon'd for Comedy, *Edward* Earl of *Oxford*; for Tragedy amongst others, *Thomas* Lord of *Buchurst*, whose *Gorboduck* is a fable, doubtless, better turn'd for Tragedy, than any on this side the *Alps* in his time; and might have been a better direction to *Shakespear* and *Ben. Johnson* than any guide they have had the luck to follow. *Here*

* *Skelton.*

Here is a King, the Queen, and their two Sons. The King divides his Realm, and gives it betwixt his two Sons. They quarrel. The Elder Brother Kills the Younger. Which provokes the Mother to Kill the Elder. Thereupon the King Kills the Mother, And then to make a clear Stage the people rise and dispatch old Gorboduck.

It is objected by our Neighbours against the English, that we delight in bloody spectacles. Our Poets who have not imitated *Gorboduck* in the regularity and roundness of the design, have not failed on the Theatre to give us the *atrocité* and blood, enough in all Conscience. From this time Dramatick Poetry began to thrive with us, and flourish wonderfully. The French confess they had nothing in this kind considerable till 1635. that the Academy Royal was founded. Long before which time we had from *Shakespear*, *Fletcher*, and *Ben. Johnson* whole Volumes; at this day in possession of the Stage, and acted with greater applause than ever. Yet after all, I fear what *Quintilian* pronounced concerning the Roman Comedy, may as justly be said of English Tragedy: *In Tragœdia maxime claudicamus, vix levem consequimur umbram.* In Tragedy we come short extreamly; hardly have we a slender shadow of it. CHAP.

CHAP. V.

Othello. More of a piece. In Tragedy four parts. Fable, the Poets part. Cinthio's *Novels.* Othello *altered for the worse. Marriage, absurd, forbidden by* Horace. *Fable of* Othello. *Use and Application.* Othello's *Love powder. High-German Doctor.* Venetians *odd taste of things. Their Women fools. Employ Strangers. Hate the Moors.* Characters. *Nothing of the Moor in* Othello, *of a Venetian in* Desdemona. *Of a Souldier in* Jago. *The Souldiers Character, by* Horace. *What by* Shakespear. Agamemnon. *Venetians no sense of Jealousie. Thoughts, in* Othello, *in a Horse, or Mastiff, more sensibly exprest. Ill Manners. Outragious to a Nobleman, to Humanity. Address, in telling bad news. In Princes Courts. In* Aristophanes. *In* Rabelais. *Venetian Senate. Their Wisdom.*

FRom all the Tragedies acted on our English Stage, *Othello* is said to bear the Bell away. The *Subject* is more of a piece, and there is indeed something like, there is, as it were, some phantom of a *Fable*. The *Fable* is always accounted the *Soul* of Tragedy. And it is the *Fable* which is properly the *Poets* part. Because the other three parts of Tragedy, to wit the *Cha-racters* are taken from the Moral Philosopher; the *thoughts* or fence, from them that teach *Rhetorick*: And the laſt part, which is the *expreſſion*, we learn from the Grammarians.

This Fable is drawn from a Novel, compos'd in Italian by *Giraldi Cinthio*, who alſo was a Writer of Tragedies. And to that uſe employ'd ſuch of his Tales, as he judged proper for the Stage. But with this of the *Moor*, he meddl'd no farther.

Shakeſpear alters it from the Original in ſeveral particulars, but always, unfortunately, for the worſe. He beſtows a name on his *Moor*; and ſtyles him the Moor of *Venice*: a Note of pre-eminence, which neither Hiſtory nor Heraldry can allow him. *Cinthio*, who knew him beſt, and whoſe creature he was, calls him ſimply a *Moor*. We ſay the Piper of *Strasburgh*; the Jew of *Florence*; And, if you pleaſe, the Pindar of *Wakefield*: all upon Record, and memorable in their Places. But we ſee no ſuch Cauſe for the *Moors* preferment to that dignity. And it is an affront to all Chroniclers, and Antiquaries, to top upon 'um a *Moor*, with that mark of renown, who yet had never faln within the Sphere of their Cogniſance.

Then

Then is the Moors *Wife*, from a simple Citizen, in *Cinthio*, dress'd up with her Top knots, and rais'd to be *Desdemona*, a Senators Daughter. All this is very strange; And therefore pleases such as reflect not on the improbability. This match might well be without the Parents Consent. Old *Horace* long ago forbad the Banes.

Sed non ut placidis Coeant immitia, non ut
Serpentes avibus geminentur, tigribus agni.

The Fable.

*O*Thello, *a Blackmoor Captain, by talking of his Prowess and Feats of War, makes* Desdemona *a Senators Daughter to be in love with him; and to be married to him, without her Parents knowledge: And having preferred* Cassio, *to be his Lieutenant, (a place which his Ensign* Jago *sued for)* Jago *in revenge, works the Moor into a Jealousy that* Cassio *Cuckolds him: which he effects by stealing and conveying a certain Handkerchief, which had, at the Wedding, been by the Moor presented to his Bride. Hereupon,* Othello *and* Jago *plot the Deaths*

(89)

of Desdemona *and* Cassio, Othello *Murders her, and soon after is convinced of her Innocence. And as he is about to be carried to Prison, in order to be punish'd for the Murder, He kills himself.*

What ever rubs or difficulty may stick on the Bark, the Moral, sure, of this Fable is very instructive.

1. First, This may be a caution to all Maidens of Quality how, without their Parents consent, they run away with Blackamoors.

Di non si accompagnare con huomo, cui la natura & il cielo, & il modo della vita, disgiunge da noi. Cinthio.

Secondly, This may be a warning to all good Wives, that they look well to their Linnen.

Thirdly, This may be a lesson to Husbands, that before their Jealousie be Tragical, the proofs may be Mathematical.

Cinthio affirms that *She was not overcome by a Womanish Appetite, but by the Vertue of the Moor.* It must be a good-natur'd Reader that takes *Cinthio*'s word in this case, tho' in a Novel. *Shakespear*, who is accountable both to the *Eyes,* and to the *Ears,* And to convince the very heart of an Audience, shews that *Desdemona* was

won,

won, by hearing *Othello* talk,
   Othello.

----I spake of most disastrous chances,
of Moving accidents, by flood and field;
of hair-breadth scapes i'th' imminent deadly
of being taken by the insolent foe;   (breach;
and sold to slavery: of my redemption thence;
and portents in my Travels History:
wherein of Antars vast, and Desarts idle,
rough Quarries, Rocks, and Hills, whose heads
                              (touch Heaven,
It was my hint to speak, such was my process:
and of the Cannibals *that each others eat:*
the Anthropophagi, *and men whose heads*
do grow beneath their shoulders----

This was the Charm, this was the philtre, the love-powder that took the Daughter of this Noble Venetian. This was sufficient to make the Black-amoor White, and reconcile all, tho' there had been a Cloven-foot into the bargain.

A meaner woman might be as soon taken by *Aqua Tetrachymagogon.*

Nodes, Cataracts, Tumours, Chilblains, Carnosity, *Shankers,* or any *Cant* in the Bill of an High-German Doctor is as good *fustian Circumstance,* and
                                        as

as likely to charm a Senators Daughter. But, it seems, the noble Venetians have an other fence of things. The *Doge* himself tells us;

Doge. I think this Tale wou'd win my Daughter too.

Horace tells us,

Intererit Multum------
Colchus an Aſſyrius, Thebis nutritus, an
Argis.

Shakeſpear in this Play calls 'em the *ſu perſubtle venetians*. Yet examine throughout the Tragedy there is nothing in the noble *Deſdemona,* that is not below any Countrey Chamber-maid with us.

And the account he gives of their Noblemen and Senate, can only be calculated for the latitude of *Gotham.*

The Character of that State is to employ ſtrangers in their Wars; But ſhall a Poet thence fancy that they will ſet a Negro to be their General; or truſt a *Moor* to defend them againſt the *Turk*? With us a Black-a moor might riſe to be a Trumpeter; but *Shakeſpear* would not have him leſs than a
Lieutenant

Lieutenant-General. With us a *Moor* might marry some little drab, or Small-coal Wench: *Shake-spear*, would provide him the Daughter and Heir of some great Lord, or Privy-Councellor: And all the Town should reckon it a very suitable match: Yet the English are not bred up with that hatred and aversion to the *Moors*, as are the Venetians, who suffer by a perpetual Hostility from them,

Littora littoribus contraria ---

Nothing is more odious in Nature than an improbable lye; And, certainly, never was any Play fraught, like this of *Othello*, with improbabilities.

The *Characters* or Manners, which are the second part in a Tragedy, are not less unnatural and improper, than the Fable was improbable and absurd.

Othello is made a Venetian General. We see nothing done by him, nor related concerning him, that comports with the condition of a General, or, indeed, of a Man, unless the killing himself, to avoid a death the Law was about to inflict upon him. When his Jealousy had wrought him up to a resolution of's taking revenge for the
sup-

suppos'd injury, He sets *Jago* to the fighting part, to kill *Cassio*; And chuses himself to murder the silly Woman his Wife, that was like to make no resistance.

His Love and his Jealousie are no part of a Souldiers Character, unless for Comedy.

But what is most intolerable is *Jago*. He is no Black-amoor Souldier, so we may be sure he should be like other Souldiers of our acquaintance; yet never in Tragedy, nor in Comedy, nor in Nature was a Souldier with his Character; take it in the Authors own words;

Fm. ---*some Eternal Villain,*
Some busie, and insinuating Rogue,
Some cogging, couzening Slave, to get some Office.

Horace Describes a Souldier otherwise:

Impiger, iracundus, inexorabilis, acer.

Shakespear knew his Character of *Jago* was inconsistent. In this very Play he pronounces,

If thou dost deliver more or less than Truth,
Thou art no Souldier.

This he knew, but to entertain the Audience with something new and surprising, against common sense, and Nature, he would pass upon us a close, dissembling, false, insinuating rascal, instead of an openhearted, frank, plain-dealing Souldier, a character constantly worn by them for some thousands of years in the World.

* *Tiberius Cæsar* had a Poet Arraign'd for his Life: because *Agamemnon* was brought on the Stage by him, with a character unbecoming a Souldier.

Our *Ensigns* and Subalterns, when disgusted by the Captain, throw up their Commissions, bluster, and are bare-fac'd. *Jago*, I hope, is not brought on the Stage, in a Red-Coat. I know not what Livery the Venetians wear: but am sure they hold not these conditions to be *alla soldatesca*.

Non sia egli per fare la vendetta con insidie, ma con la spada in mano. Cinthio.

Nor is our Poet more discreet in his *Desdemona*, He had chosen a Souldier for his Knave: And a Venetian Lady is to be the Fool.

This Senators Daughter runs away to

* *Sueton* in Tib.

(a Carriers Inn) the *Sagittary*, with a Black-amoor: is no sooner wedded to him, but the very night she Beds him, is importuning and teizing him for a young smock-fac'd Lieutenant, *Cassio*. And tho' she perceives the *Moor* Jealous of *Cassio*, yet will she not forbear, but still rings *Cassio, Cassio* in both his Ears.

Roderigo is the Cully of *Jago*, brought in to be murder'd by *Jago*, that *Jago*'s hands might be the more in Blood, and be yet the more abominable Villain: who without that was too wicked on all Conscience; And had more to answer for, than any Tragedy, or Furies could inflict upon him. So there can be nothing in the *characters*, either for the profit, or to delight an Audience.

The third thing to be consider'd is the *Thoughts*. But from such *Characters*, we need not expect many that are either true, or fine, or noble.

And without these, that is, without sense or meaning, the fourth part of Tragedy, which is the *expression* can hardly deserve to be treated on distinctly. The verse rumbling in our Ears are of good use to help off the action.

In the *Neighing* of an Horse, or in the
growling

growling of a Mastiff, there is a meaning, there is as lively expression, and, may I say, more humanity, than many times in the Tragical flights of *Shakespear*.

Step then amongst the Scenes to observe the Conduct in this Tragedy.

The first we see are *Jago* and *Roderigo*, by Night in the Streets of *Venice*. After growling a long time together, they resolve to tell *Brabantio* that his Daughter is run away with the Black-a-moor. *Jago* and *Roderigo* were not of quality to be familiar with *Brabantio*, nor had any provocation from him, to deserve a rude thing at their hands. *Brabantio* was a Noble Venetian one of the Sovereign Lords, and principal persons in the Government, Peer to the most Serene *Doge*, one attended with more state, ceremony and punctillio, than any English Duke, or Nobleman in the Government will pretend to. This misfortune in his Daughter is so prodigious, so tender a point, as might puzzle the finest Wit of the most *superfubtle* Venetian to touch upon it, or break the discovery to her Father. See then how delicately *Shakespear* minces the matter:

Rod. *What ho*, Brabantio, *Signior* Brabantio, *ho*.

Jago.

Jago. *Awake, what ho,* Brabantio,
Thieves, thieves, thieves:
Look to your House, your Daughter, and your Bags
Thieves, thieves.

Brabantio at a Window.

Bra. *What is the reason of this terrible summons?*
What is the matter there?

Rod. *Signior, is all your Family within?*
Jago. *Are your Doors lockt?*
Bra. *Why, wherefore ask you this?*
your Gown,

Jago. *Sir, you are robb'd, for shame put on*
Your Heart is burst, you have lost half your Soul,
Even now, very now, an old black Ram
Is tupping your white Ewe: arise, arise,
Awake the snorting Citizens with the Bell,
Or else the Devil will make a Grandsire of
you, arise I sad.

Nor have they yet done, amongst other ribaldry, they tell him.

Jago. *Sir, you are one of those that will not serve God, if the Devil bid you; because we come to do you service, you think us Ruffians, you'le have your Daughter covered with a Barbary Stallion. You'le have your Nephews*

H *neigh*

neigh to you; you'le have Courfers for Coufins, and Gennets for Germans.

Bra. *What prophane wretch art thou?*

Jago. *I am one, Sir, that come to tell you, your Daughter and the Moor, are now making the Beaſt with two backs.*

In former days there wont to be kept at the Courts of Princes ſome body in a Fools Coat, that in pure ſimplicity might let ſlip ſomething, which made way for the ill news, and blunted the ſhock, which otherwiſe might have come too violent upon the party.

Ariſtophanes puts *Nicias* and *Demoſthenes* in the diſguiſe of Servants, that they might, without indecency, be Drunk; And Drunk he muſt make them that they might without reſerve lay open the *Arcana* of State; And the Knavery of their *Miniſters*.

After King *Francis* had been taken Priſoner at *Pavia*. *Rabelais* tells of a Drunken bout between *Gargantua* and *Fryer John*; where the valiant Fryer, bragging over his Cups, amongſt his other flights, ſays he, *Had I liv'd in the days of Jeſus Chriſt, I would ha' guarded* Mount Olivet *that the Jews ſhould never ha' tane him, The Devil fetch me, if I would not have ham-*

ham string'd those Mr. Apostles, that after their good Supper, ran away so scurvily and left their Master to shift for himself. I hate a Man should run away, when he should play at sharps. 'Pox on't, that I shou'd not be King of France for an hundred years or two. I wou'd curtail all our French Dogs that ran away at Pavia.

This is addreſs, this is truly Satyr, where the preparation is ſuch, that the thing principally deſign'd, falls in, as it only were of courſe.

But *Shakeſpear* ſhews us another ſort of addreſs, his manners and good breeding muſt not be like the reſt of the Civil World. *Brabantio* was not in Maſquerade, was not *incognito*; *Jago* well knew his rank and dignity.

Jago, *The* Magnifico *is much beloved,*
And hath in his effect, a voice potential
As double as the Duke ------

But beſides the Manners to a *Magnifico*, humanity cannot bear that an old Gentleman in his misfortune ſhould be inſulted over with ſuch a rabble of Skoundrel language, when no cauſe or provocation. Yet thus it is on our Stage, this is our

School of good manners, and the *Speculum Vitæ*.

But our *Magnifico* is here in the dark, nor are yet his Robes on: attend him to the Senate houſe, and there ſee the difference, ſee the effects of Purple.

So, by and by, we find the Duke of *Venice* with his Senators in Councel, at Midnight, upon advice that the Turks, or Ottamites, or both together, were ready in tranſport Ships, put to Sea, in order to make a Deſcent upon *Cyprus*. This is the poſture, when we ſee *Brabantio*, and *Othello* join them. By their Conduct and manner of talk, a body muſt ſtrain hard to fancy the Scene at *Venice*; And not rather in ſome of our Cinq-ports, where the Baily and his Fiſher-men are knocking their heads together on account of ſome Whale; or ſome terrible broil upon the Coaſt. But to ſhew them true Venetians, the Maritime affairs ſtick not long on their hand; the publick may ſink or ſwim. They will ſit up all night to hear a Doctors Commons, Matrimonial, Cauſe. And have the Merits of the Cauſe at large laid open to 'em, that they may decide it before they Stir. What can be pleaded to keep awake their attention ſo wonderfully?

Never

Never, sure, was *form* of *pleading* so tedious and so heavy, as this whole Scene, and midnight entertainment. Take his own words: says the *Respondent*.

Oth. *Most potent, grave, and reverend Signiors,*
My very noble, and approv'd good Masters:
That I have tane away this old mans Daughter;
It is most true: true, I have Married her,
The very front and head of my offending,
Hath this extent, no more: rude I am in my
speech.
And little blest with the set phrase of peace,
For since these Arms of mine had seven years pith,
Till now some nine Moons wasted, they have us'd
Their dearest action in the Tented Field:
And little of this great World can I speak,
More than pertains to Broils and Battail,
And therefore little shall I grace my Cause,
In speaking of my self; yet by your gracious patience
I would a round unravish'd Tale deliver,
Of my whole course of love, what drugs, what charms
What Conjuration, and what mighty Magick,
(for such proceedings am I charg'd withal)
I won his Daughter.

All this is but *Preamble*, to tell the Court that He wants words. This was the Eloquence

H 3

quence which kept them up all Night, and drew their attention, in the midst of their alarms.

One might rather think the novelty, and strangeness of the case prevail'd upon them: no, the Senators do not reckon it strange at all. Instead of starting at the Prodigy, every one is familiar with *Desdemona*, as he were her own natural Father, rejoice in her good fortune, and wish their own several Daughters as hopefully married. Should the Poet have provided such a Husband for an only Daughter of any noble Peer in *England*, the Black-amoor must have chang'd his Skin, to look our House of Lords in the Face.

Æschylus is noted in *Aristophanes* for letting *Niobe* be two or three *Acts* on the Stage, before she speaks. Our Noble Venetian, sure, is in the other more unnatural extreme. His words flow in abundance; no Butter-Quean can be more lavish. Nay: he is for talking of State-Affairs too, above any body:

Bra. *Please it your Grace, on to the State Affairs*----

Yet is this *Brabantio* sensible of his affliction;

fliction; before the end of the Play his Heart breaks, he dies.

Gra. Poor Desdemona, *I am glad thy Father's dead,*
Thy match was mortal to him, and pure grief
Shore his old thread in twain----

A third part in a Tragedy is the *Thoughts*: from Venetians, Noblemen, and Senators, we may expect fine *Thoughts*. Here is a tryal of skill: for a parting blow, the *Duke*, and *Brabantio* Cap *sentences*. Where then shall we seek for the *Thoughts*, if we let flip this occasion? says the Duke:

Duk: Let me speak like your self and lay a Sentence,
Which like a greese or step, may help these lovers
Into your favour.
When remedies are past the grief is ended,
By seeing the worst which late on hopes depended,
To mourn a mischief that is past and gone,
Is the next way to draw more mischief on;
What cannot be preserv'd when Fortune takes,
Patience her injury a Mocker makes.
The rob'd that smiles, steals something from a
(*Thief,*
He robs himself that spends an hopeless grief.

Bra.

Bra. *So let the Turk of Cyprus us beguile*
We lose it not so long as we can smile;
He bears the sentence well, that nothing bears
But the free comfort which from thence he hears,
But he bears both the sentence and the sorrow,
That to pay grief must of poor patience borrow:
These Sentences *to Sugar,* or *to Gall,*
Being strong on both sides are equivocal.
But words are words, I never yet did hear,
That the bruis'd Heart was pierced through the Ear.
Beseech you now to the affairs of State.

How far wou'd the Queen of *Sheba* have travell'd to hear the Wisdom of our Noble Venetians? or is not our * *Brentford* a *Venetian* Colony, for methinks their talk is the very same?

What says Prince *Volscius* ?
  Volscius.
What shall I do, what conduct shall I find
To lead me through this twy light of my mind?

What says *Amaryllis* ?
  Ama. *I hope its slow beginning will portend*
A forward exit to all future end.
  Rehearsal.

What

What says Prince *Pretty-man*?

*Pre. Was ever Son yet brought to this distress,
To be, for being a Son, made Fatherless?
Ah, you just Gods, rob me not of a Father,
The being of a Son take from me rather.*

Panurge, sadly perplexed, and trying all the means in the World, to be well advised, in that knotty point *whether he should Marry, or no*; Amongst the rest, consults *Raminigrobis,* an old Poet; as one belonging to *Apollo*; And from whom he might expect something like an Oracle. And he was not disappointed. From *Raminigrobis* he had this Answer:

> *Prenez la, ne la prenez pas.
> Si vous la prenez, c'est bien fait.
> Si ne la prenez, en effet
> Ce sera ouvre par compas.
> Gallopez, mais allez le pas.
> Recullez, entrés y de fait.*
>   *Prenez la, ne.*

> *Take, or not take her, off or on;
> Handy dandy is your Lot.
> When her name you write, you blot.*

Tis

'Tis undone, when all is done,
Ended, ere it is begun.
Never Gallop whilst you Trot.
Set not forward, when you run,
Nor be single, tho' alone,
Take, or not take her, off, or on.

What provocation, or cause of malice our Poet might have to Libel the most *Serene Republick*, I cannot tell: but certainly, there can be no wit in this representation.

For the *Second Act*, our Poet having dispatcht his affairs at *Venice*, shews the Action next (I know not how many leagues off) in the Island of *Cyprus*. The Audience must be there too: And yet our *Bays* had it never in his head, to make any provision of Transport Ships for them.

In the days that the *Old Testament* was Acted in *Clerkenwell*, by the *Parish Clerks* of *London*, the Israelites might pass through the *Red sea*: but alas, at this time, we have no *Moses* to bid the Waters *make way*, and to Usher us along. Well, the absurdities of this kind break no Bones. They may make Fools of us; but do not hurt our Morals.

Come a shoar then, and observe the

Countenance of the People, after the dreadful Storm, and their apprehensions from an Invasion by the Ottomites, their succour and friends scatter'd and tost, no body knew whither. The first that came to Land was *Cassio*, his first Salutation to the Governour, *Montanio*, is:

Cas. *Thanks to the valiant of this Isle:*
That so approve the Moor, and let the Heavens
Give him defence against their Elements,
For I have lost him on the dangerous Sea.

To him the Governour speaks, indeed, like a Man in his wits.

Mont. *Is he well Shipt?*

The Lieutenant answers thus.

Cas. *His Bark is stoutly Tymber'd, and his Pilot*
Of very expert, and approv'd allowance,
Therefore my hopes (not surfeited to death)
Stand in bold care.

The Governours first question was very proper; his next question, in this posture of affairs, is:

Mont.

Mont. But, good Lieutenant, is our general Wiv'd?

A question so remote, so impertinent and absurd, so odd and surprising never entered *Bayes's Pericranium.* Only the answer may Tally with it.

Cas. Most fortunately, he hath atcheiv'd a Maid,
That Parragons description, and wild fame:
One that excels the quirks of blasoning Pens:
And in the essential vesture of Creation,
Does bear an excellency----

They who like this Authors writing will not be offended to find so much repeated from him. I pretend not here to tax either the *Sense,* or the *Language*; those *Circumstances* had their proper place in the Venetian Senate. What I now cite is to shew how probable, how natural, how reasonable the Conduct is, all along.

I thought it enough that *Cassio* should be acquainted with a Virgin of that rank and consideration in *Venice,* as *Desdemona.* I wondred that in the Senate-house every one should know her so familiarly: yet,

here

here also at *Cyprus*, every body is in a rapture at the name of *Desdemona*: except only *Montanio* who must be ignorant; that *Cassio*, who has an excellent cut in shaping an Answer, may give him the satisfaction:

Mont. *What is she?*

Cas. *She that I spoke of: our Captains Captain,*
Left in the Condnct of the bold Jago,
Whose footing here anticipates our thoughts
A Sennets speed: great Jove *Othello guard,*
And swell his Sail with thine own powerful breath.
That he may bless this Bay with his Tall Ship,
And swiftly come to Desdemona's *Arms,*
Give renewed fire to our extincted Spirits,
And bring all Cyprus *comfort:*

      Enter Desdemona, &c.

-----*O behold,*
The riches of the Ship is come on shoar.
Ye men of Cyprus, *let her have your Knees:*
Hail to the Lady: and the Grace of Heaven
Before, behind thee, and on every hand.
Enwheel the round----

         In

In the name of phrenzy, what means this Souldier? or would he talk thus, if he meant any thing at all? Who can say *Shakespear* is to blame in his *Character* of a Souldier? Has he not here done him reason? When cou'd our *Tramontains* talk at this rate? but our *Jarsey* and *Garnsey* Captains must not speak so fine things, nor compare with the Mediterranean, or Garisons in *Rhodes* and *Cyprus*.

The next thing our Officer does, is to salute *Jago*'s Wife, with this *Congé* to the Husband,

Caf. *Good Ancient, you are welcome, welcome Mistriss,*
Let it not Gall your Patience, good Jago,
That I extend my Manners, 'tis my Breeding,
That gives me this bold shew of Curtesy.

Jago. *Sir, would she give you so much of her lips,*
As of her tongue she has bestow'd on me,
You'd have enough.

Def. *Alass! she has no speech.*

Now follows a long rabble of Jack-pudden farce betwixt *Jago* and *Desdemona*, that runs on with all the little plays, jingle,
and

and trash below the patience of any Countrey Kitchin-maid with her Sweet-heart. The Venetian *Donna* is hard put to't for paftime! And this is all, when they are newly got on fhoar, from a difmal Tempeft, and when every moment fhe might expect to hear her Lord (as fhe calls him) that fhe runs fo mad after, is arriv'd or loft. And moreover.

---*In a Town of War,*
---*The peoples Hearts brimful of fear.*

Never in the World had any Pagan Poet his Brains turn'd at this Monftrous rate. But the ground of all this Bedlam-Buffoonry we faw, * in the cafe of the French *Strolers*, the Company for Acting *Chrifts Paffion*, or the *Old Teftament*, were Carpenters, Coblers, and illiterate fellows; who found that the Drolls, and Fooleries interlarded by them, brought in the rabble, and lengthened their time, fo they got Money by the bargain.

Our *Shakefpear*, doubtlefs, was a great Mafter in this craft. Thefe Carpenters and Coblers were the guides he followed. And it is then no wonder that we find fo much

*Page 54.

farce,

farce and *Apocryphal Matter* in his Tragedies. Thereby un-hallowing the Theatre, profaning the name of Tragedy; And instead of representing Men and Manners, turning all Morality, good sence, and humanity into mockery and derision.

But pass we to something of a more serious air and Complexion. *Othello* and his Bride are the first Night, no sooner warm in Bed together, but a Drunken Quarrel happening in the Garison, two Souldiers Fight; And the General rises to part the Fray: He swears.

Othel. *Now by Heaven,*
My blood begins my safer guides to rule,
And passion, having my best judgment cool'd,
Assays to lead the way: if once I stir,
Or do but lift this arm, the best of you
Shall sink in my rebuke: give me to know
How this foul rout began; who set it on,
And he that is approv'd in this offence,
Tho' he had twin'd with me both at a birth,
Should lose me: what, in a Town of War,
Yet wild, the peoples Hearts brimful of fear,
To manage private, and domestick quarrels,
In Night, and on the Court, and guard of safety,
'Tis Monstrous, Jago, *who began?*

In

In the days of yore, Souldiers did not fwear in this fashion. What should a Souldier say farther, when he swears, unless he blaspheme? action shou'd speak the rest. What follows must be *ex ore gladii*; He is to rap out an Oath, not Wire-draw and Spin it out: by the style one might judge that *Shakespears* Souldiers were never bred in a Camp, but rather had belong'd to some Affidavit-Office. Consider also throughout this whole Scene, how the Moorish General proceeds in examining into this *Rout*; No Justice *Clod-pate* could go on with more Phlegm and deliberation. The very first night that he lyes with the *Divine Desdemona* to be thus interrupted, might provoke a Mans Christian Patience to swear in another style. But a Negro General is a Man of strange Mettle. Only his Venetian Bride is a match for him. She understands that the Souldiers in the Garison are by th'ears together: And presently she at midnight, is in amongst them.

Desd. *What's the matter there?*
Othel. *All's well now Sweeting----*
    Come away to Bed.---

In the beginning of this *second Act*, before

fore they had lain together, *Desdemona* was said to be, *oar Captains Captain*; Now they are no sooner in Bed together, but *Jago* is advising *Cassio* in these words.

Jago. ----*Our Generals Wife is now the General, I may say so in this respect, for that he hath devoted, and given up himself to the contemplation, mark, and devotement of her parts and graces. Confess your self freely to her, importune her; she'll help to put you in your place again: she is so free, so kind, so apt, so blessed a disposition, that she holds it a vice in her goodness, not to do more than she is requested. This broken joint between you and her Husband, intreat her to splinter---*

And he says afterwards.

Jago. ----*'Tis most easie*
The inclining Desdemona *to subdue,*
In any honest suit. She's fram'd as fruitful,
As the free Elements: And then for her
To win the Moor, were't to renounce his Baptism,
All seals and symbols of redeemed sin,
His soul is so enfetter'd to her love,
That she may make, unmake, do what she list:
Even as her appetite shall play the God
With his weak function---

This

This kind of discourse implies an experienc'd and long conversation, the Honey-Moon over, and a Marriage of some standing. Would any man, in his wits, talk thus of a Bridegroom and Bride the first night of their coming together?

Yet this is necessary for our Poet; it would not otherwise serve his turn. This is the source, the foundation of his Plot; hence is the spring and occasion for all the Jealousie and bluster that ensues.

Nor are we in better circumstances for *Roderigo*. The last thing said by him in the former *Act* was,

Rod. —*I'll go sell all my Land.*

A fair Estate is sold to *put money in his Purse,* for this adventure. And lo here, the next day.

Rod. *I do follow here in the Chace, not like a Hound that hunts, but one that fills up the cry: My Money is almost spent. I have been tonight exceedingly well cudgell'd, I think the issue will be, I shall have so much experience for my pains, and so no Money at all, and with a little more wit return to Venice.*

The Venetian squire had a good riddance for his Acres. The Poet allows him just time to be once drunk, a very conscionable reckoning!

In this *Second Act*, the face of affairs could in truth be no other, than

---In a Town of War,
Yet wild, the peoples Hearts brim-ful of fear.

But nothing either in this *Act*, or in the rest that follow, shew any colour or complexion, any resemblance or proportion to that face and posture it ought to bear. Should a Painter draw any one *Scene* of this Play, and write over it, *This is a Town of War*; would any body believe that the Man were in his senses? would not a *Goose*, or *Dromedary* for it, be a name as just and suitable? And what in Painting would be absurd, can never pass upon the World for Poetry.

Cassio having escaped the Storm comes on shoar at *Cyprus*, that night gets Drunk, Fights, is turn'd out from his Command, grows sober again, takes advice how to be restor'd, is all Repentance and Mortification: yet before he sleeps, is in the Morning at his Generals door with a noise of Fiddles,
and

and a Droll to introduce him to a little Mouth-speech with the Bride.

Cassio. *Give me advantage of some brief*
(*discourse*
With Desdemona *alone.*
Em. *Pray you come in,*
I will bestow you, where you shall have time
To speak your bosom freely.

So, they are put together: And when he had gone on a good while *speaking his bosom,* Desdemona answers him.

Des. *Do not doubt that, before* Emilia *here,*
I give thee warrant of thy place; assure thee,
If I do vow a friendship, I'll perform it,
To the last article ---

Then after a ribble rabble of fulsome impertinence. She is at her Husband slap dash:

Desd. --*Good love, call him back.*
Othel. *Not now, sweet* Desdemona, *some*
(*other time.*
Desd. *But shall't shortly?*
Othel. *The sooner, sweet, for you.*
Desd. *Shall't be to-night at Supper?*

Othel. *No, not tonight.*

Desd. *To-Morrow Dinner then?*

Othel. *I shall not dine at home,
I meet the Captains at the Citadel.*

Desd. *Why then to morrow night, or Tuesday
(morn,
Or night, or Wednesday morn?*

After forty lines more, at this rate, they part, and then comes the wonderful Scene, where *Jago* by shrugs, half words, and ambiguous reflections, works *Othello* up to be Jealous. One might think, after what we have seen, that there needs no great cunning, no great poetry and address to make the *Moor* Jealous. Such impatience, such a rout for a handsome young fellow, the very morning after her Marriage must make him either to be jealous, or to take her for a *Changeling*, below his Jealousie. After this *Scene*, it might strain the Poets skill to reconcile the couple, and allay the Jealousie. *Jago* now can only *actum agere*, and vex the audience with a nauseous repetition.

Whence comes it then, that this is the top scene, the Scene that raises *Othello* above all other Tragedies on our Theatres? It is purely from the *Action*, from the

Mops,

Mops and the Mows, the Grimace, the Grins and Gesticulation. Such scenes as this have made all the World run after *Harlequim* and *Scaramuccio*.

The several degrees of *Action* were amongst the Ancients distinguish'd by the *Cothurnus*, the *Soccus*, and by the *Planipes*.

Had this scene been represented at old *Rome*, *Othello* and *Jago* must have quitted their Buskins; They must have played *barefoot*: the spectators would not have been content without seeing their Podometry; And the Jealousie work at the very Toes of 'em. Words, be they Spanish, or Polish, or any inarticulate sound, have the same effect, they can only serve to distinguish, and, as it were, beat time to the *Action*. But here we see a known Language does wofully encumber, and clog the operation: as either forc'd, or heavy, or trifling, or incoherent, or improper, or most what improbable. When no words interpose to spoil the conceipt, every one interprets as he likes best. So in that memorable dispute betwixt *Panurge* and our English Philosopher in *Rabelais*, perform'd without a word speaking; The Theologians, Physicians, and Surgeons, made one inference; the Lawyers, Civilians, and Canonists, drew

another

another conclusion more to their mind.

Othello the night of his arrival at *Cyprus*, is to consummate with *Desdemona*, they go to Bed. Both are rais'd and run into the Town amidst the Souldiers that were a fighting: then go to Bed again, that morning he sees *Cassio* with her; She importunes him to restore *Cassio*. *Othello* shews nothing of the Souldiers Mettle: but like a tedious, drawling, tame Goose, is gaping after any paultrey Insinuation, labouring to be jealous; And catching at every blown surmize.

Jago. *My Lord, I see you are moved.*
Oth. *No, not much moved.*
Do not think but Desdemona *is honest.*
Jag. *Long live she so, and long live you to think*
(so.
Oth. *And yet how Nature erring from it self,*
Jag. *I, There's the point: as to be bold with you,*
Not to affect many proposed Matches
Of her own clime, complexion, and degree,
Wherein we see, in all things, Nature tends,
Fye, we may smell in such a will most rank,
Foul disproportion, thoughts unnatural—

The Poet here is certainly in the right, and by consequence the foundation of the Play must

must be concluded to be Monstrous; And the constitution, all over, to be *most rank, Foul disproportion, thoughts unnatural.*

Which instead of moving pity, or any passion Tragical and Reasonable, can produce nothing but horror and aversion, and what is odious and grievous to an Audience. After this fair Mornings work, the Bride enters, drops a Cursey.

Desd. How now, my dear Othello,
*Your Dinner, and the generous Islanders
By you invited, do attend your presence.*
Oth. *I am to blame.*
Desd. *Why is your speech so faint? Are you not well?*
Oth. *I have a pain upon my Fore-head, dear.*

Michael Cassio came not from *Venice* in the Ship with *Desdemona*, nor till this Morning could be suspected of an opportunity with her. And 'tis now but Dinner time; yet the *Moor* complains of his Forehead. He might have set a Guard on *Cassio*, or have lockt up *Desdemona*, or have observ'd their carriage a day or two longer. He is on other occasions phlegmatick enough:

enough: this is very hasty. But after Dinner we have a wonderful flight:

Othel. *What sense had I of her stoln hours of lust?*
I saw't not, thought it not, it harm'd not me:
I slept the next night well, was free and merry,
I found not Cassio's *kisses on her lips*---

A little after this, says he,

Oth. *Give me a living reason that she's disloyal.*
Jago. ---*I lay with* Cassio *lately,*
And being troubled with a raging Tooth, I could not sleep;
There are a kind of men so loose of Soul,
That in their sleeps will mutter their affairs,
One of this kind is Cassio:
In sleep I heard him say: sweet Desdemona,
Let us be wary, let us hide our loves.
And then, Sir, wou'd he gripe, and wring my hand,
Cry out, sweet Creature; and then kiss me hard,
As if he pluckt up kisses by the roots,
That grew upon my Lips, then laid his Leg
Over my Thigh, and sigh'd, and kiss'd, and then
Cry'd, cursed fate, that gave thee to the Moor.

By

By the Rapture of *Othello*, one might think that he raves, is not of sound Memory, forgets that he has not yet been two nights in the Matrimonial Bed with his *Desdemona*. But we find *Jago*, who should have a better memory, forging his lies after the very same Model. The very night of their Marriage at *Venice*, the Moor, and also *Cassio*, were sent away to *Cyprus*. In the *Second Act*, *Othello* and his Bride go the first time to Bed; The *Third Act* opens the next morning. The parties have been in view to this moment. We saw the opportunity which was given for *Cassio* to *speak his bosom* to her, *once*, indeed, might go a great way with a Venetian. But *once*, will not do the Poets business; The *Audience* must suppose a great many bouts, to make the plot operate. They must deny their senses, to reconcile it to common sense: or make it any way consistent, and hang together.

Nor, for the most part, are the single thoughts more consistent, than is the œconomy: The Indians do as they ought in painting the Devil White: but says *Othello*:

Oth. ---- *Her name that was as fresh*
As Dian*'s Visage, is now begrim'd and black,*
As mine own face ---
           There

There is not a Monky but underſtands Nature better ; not a Pug in *Barbary* that has not a truer taſte of things.

Othel. ---- *O now for ever*
Farewel the tranquil mind, farewel content;
Farewel the plumed troop, and the big Wars,
That make Ambition Vertue : O farewel,
Farewel the neighing Steed, and the ſhrill Trump,
The ſpirit ſtirring Drum, th' ear-piercing Fief,
The royal Banner, and all quality,
Pride, Pomp, and Circumſtance of glorious War,
And O ye Mortal Engines, whoſe wide throats
Th' immortal Joves great clamours counterfeit,
Farewel, Othello's *occupation's gone.*

Theſe lines are recited here, not for any thing Poetical in them, beſides the ſound, that pleaſes. Yet this ſort of imagery and amplification is extreamly taking, where it is juſt and natural. As in *Gorboduck*, when a young Princeſs on whoſe fancy the perſonal gallantry of the Kings Son then ſlain, had made a ſtrong impreſſion, thus, out of the abundance of her imagination, pours forth her grief:

Marcella.

Marcella: --- *Ah noble Prince! how oft have I beheld*
Thee mounted on thy fierce, and trampling Steed,
Shining in Armour bright before the Tilt,
Wearing thy Mistress sleeve ty'd on thy helm.
Then charge thy staff, to please thy Ladies Eye,
That bow'd the head piece of thy friendly Foe?
How oft in arms, on Horse to bend the Mace,
How oft in arms, on foot, to break the Spear;
Which never now these Eyes may see agen?

Notwithstanding that this Scene had proceeded with fury and bluster sufficient to make the whole Isle ring of his Jealousy, yet is *Desdemona* diverting her self with a paultry buffoon and only solicitous in quest of *Cassio* :

Desd. *Seek him, bid him come hither, tell him* ------
Where shou'd I lose that Handcherchief, Emilia *?*
Believe me I had rather lose my Purse,
Full of Crusado's : And but my noble Moor
Is true of mind, and made of no such baseness,
As Jealous Creatures are; it were enough
To put him to ill thinking.

Em.

Em. Is he not Jealous?

Desd. Who he? I think the Sun, where he was born,
Drew all such humours from him.

By this manner of speech one wou'd gather the couple had been yoak'd together a competent while, what might she say more, had they cohabited, and had been Man and Wife seven years?

She spies the Moor.

Desd. I will not leave him now,
Till Cassio is recall'd.
I have sent to bid Cassio come speak with you.
   Othel. ----Lend me thy Handkerchief.
   Desd. ---- This is a trick to put me from my suit.
I pray let Cassio be receiv'd agen.
   Em. ---Is not this man Jealous?
---'Tis not a year or two shews us a man---

As if for the first year or two, *Othello* had not been jealous? This *third Act* begins in the morning, at noon she drops the Handkerchief, after dinner she misses it, and then follows all this outrage and horrible clutter about it. If we believe a small
Damosel

Damosel in the last *Scene* of this *Act*, this day is effectually seven days.

Bianca. --- *What keep a week away! seven days, seven nights,*
Eightscore eight hours, and lovers absent hours,
More tedious than the Dial eightscore times.
Oh weary reckoning!

Our Poet is at this plunge, that whether this *Act* contains the compass of one day, of seven days, or of seven years, or of all together, the repugnance and absurdity would be the same. For *Othello*, all the while, has nothing to say or to do, but what loudly proclaim him jealous: her friend and confident *Emilia* again and again rounds her in the Ear that *the Man* is Jealous: yet this Venetian dame is neither to see, nor to hear; nor to have any sense or understanding, nor to strike any other note but *Cassio, Cassio*.

The Scotchman hearing *trut Scot, trut Scot*, when he saw it came from a Bird, checkt his Choler, and put up his *Swerd* again, with a *Braad O God, G. if thaa'dst ben a Maan, as th'art ane Green Geuse, I sud ha stuck tha' to thin heart.* *Desdemona*
and

and that Parrot might pass for *Birds of a Feather*; and if *Sauney* had not been more generous than *Othello*, but continued to insult the poor Creature after this beastly example, he would have given our Poet as good stuff to work upon: And his *Tragedy of the Green Geuse*, might have deserv'd a better audience, than this of *Desdemona*, or *The Moor of Venice*.

ACT IV.

Enter Jago *and* Othello.

Jago. *Will you think so?*
Othel. *Think so,* Jago.
Jago. *What, to kiss in private?*
Othel. *An unauthorised kiss.*
Jago. *Or to be naked with her friend a-bed, An hour or more, not meaning any harm?*
Othel. *Naked a-bed,* Jago, *and not mean harm?* -----

At this gross rate of trifling, our General and his Auncient March on most heroically; till the Jealous Booby has his Brains turn'd; and falls in a Trance. Would any imagine this to be the Language of Venetians, of Souldiers, and mighty Captains?
no

no *Bartholomew* Droll cou'd subsist upon such trash. But lo, a Stratagem never presented in Tragedy.

Jago. Stand you while a part —
— Incave your self;
And mark the Jeers, the Gibes, and notable scorns;
That dwell in every region of his face,
For I will make him tell the tale a new,
Where, how, how oft, how long ago, and when,
He has, and is again to Cope your Wife:
I say, but mark his gesture —

With this device *Othello* withdraws. Says *Jago* aside.

Jago. Now will I question Cassio *of* Bianca,
A Huswife —
That doats on Cassio *—*
He when he hears of her cannot refrain
From the excess of Laughter —
As he shall smile, Othello *shall go mad,*
And his unbookish jealousy must conster
Poor Cassio*'s smiles, gesture, and light behaviour*
Quite in the wrong —

K So

So to work they go: And *Othello* is as wise a commentator, and makes his applications pat, as heart cou'd wish ---- but I wou'd not expect to find this Scene acted nearer than in *Southwark* Fair. But the *Handkerchief* is brought in at last, to stop all holes, and close the evidence. So now being satisfied with the proof, they come to a resolution, that the offenders shall be murdered.

Othel. --- *But yet the pity of it, Jago, ah the pity.*

Jago. *If you be so fond over her iniquity give her Patent to offend. For if it touches not you, it comes near no Body.*

Do it not with poison, strangle her in her Bed; Even the Bed she has contaminated.

Oth. *Good, good, the Justice of it pleases, very good.*

Jago. *And for Cassio, let me be his undertaker ----*

Jago had some pretence to be discontent with *Othello* and *Cassio*: And what passed hitherto, was the operation of revenge. *Desdemona* had never done him harm, always kind to him, and to his Wife; was his

his Country-woman, a Dame of quality: for him to abet her Murder, shews nothing of a Souldier, nothing of a Man, nothing of Nature in it. The *Ordinary* of *New-gate* never had the like Monster to pass under his examination. Can it be any diversion to see a Rogue beyond what the Devil ever finish'd? Or wou'd it be any instruction to an Audience? *Jago* cou'd desire no better than to set *Cassio* and *Othello*, his two Enemies, by the Ears together; so he might have been reveng'd on them both at once: And chusing for his own share, the Murder of *Desdemona*, he had the opportunity to play booty, and save the poor harmless wretch. But the Poet must do every thing by contraries: to surprize the Audience still with something horrible and prodigious, beyond any human imagination. At this rate he must out-do the Devil, to be a Poet in the rank with *Shakespear*.

Soon after this, arrives from *Venice*, *Ludovico*, a noble Cousin of *Desdemona*, presently she is at him also, on the behalf of *Cassio*.

Desd. *Cousin there's fallen between him*
and my Lord
An unkind breach, but you shall make all well.
      K 2   Lud.

Lud. *Is there division 'twixt my Lord and* Caſſio.

Deſd. *A moſt unhappy one, I wou'd do much To attone them, for the love I bear to* Caſſio.

By this time, we are to believe the couple have been a week or two Married: And *Othello*'s Jealouſie that had rag'd ſo loudly, and had been ſo uneaſie to himſelf, muſt have reach'd her knowledge. The *Audience* have all heard him more plain with her, than was needful to a Venetian capacity: And yet ſhe muſt ſtill be impertinent in her ſuit for *Caſſio*, well, this *Magnifico* comes from the *Doge*, and Senators, to diſplace *Othello*.

Lud. ---*Deputing* Caſſio *in his Government.*
Deſd. *Truſt me, I am glad on't.*
Oth. *Indeed.*
Deſd. *My Lord.*
Oth. *I am glad to ſee you mad.*
Deſd. *How, ſweet* Othello.
Oth. *Devil.*
Deſd. *I have not deſerved this.*
Oth. *O Devil, Devil---*
Out of my ſight.
Deſd. *I will not ſtay to offend you.*
Lud. *Truly, an obedient Lady.*

I do

I do beseech your Lordship call her back.

  Oth. *Mistress.*

  Desd. *My Lord.*

  Oth. *What would you with her Sir?*

  Lud. *Who, I, my Lord?*

  Oth. *I, you did wish that I wou'd make her turn.*
Sir, she can turn, and turn, and yet go on,
And turn agen, and she can weep, Sir, weep.
And she is obedient, as you say, obedient:
Very obedient ----

  Lud. *What strike your Wife?*

Of what flesh and blood does our Poet make these noble Venetians? the men without Gall; the Women without either Brains or Sense? A Senators Daughter runs away with this Black-amoor; the Government employs this Moor to defend them against the Turks, so resent not the Moors Marriage at present, but the danger over, her Father gets the Moor Cashier'd, sends his Kinsman, Seignior *Ludovico*, to *Cyprus* with the Commission for a new General; who, at his arrival, finds the Moor calling the Lady his Kinswoman, Whore and Strumpet, and kicking her: what says the *Magnifico?*

Lud. My Lord this would not be believ'd in Venice,
Tho' I fhou'd fwear I faw't, 'tis very much;
Make her amends: fhe weeps.

The Moor has no body to take his part, no body of his Colour: *Ludovico* has the new Governour *Caffio*, and all his Countrymen Venetians about him. What Poet wou'd give a villanous Black-amoor this Afcendant? What Tramontain could fancy the Venetians fo low, fo defpicable, or fo patient? this outrage to an injur'd Lady, the *Divine Defdemona*, might in a colder Climate have provoked fomebody to be her Champion: but the Italians may well conclude we have a ftrange Genius for Poetry. In the next Scene *Othello* is examining the fuppofed Bawd; then follows another ftorm of horrour and outrage againft the poor Chicken, his Wife. Some Drayman or drunken Tinker might poffibly treat his drab at this fort of rate, and mean no harm by it: but for his excellency, a My-lord General, to Serenade a Senator's Daughter with fuch a volly of fcoundrel filthy Language, is fure the moft abfurd Maggot that ever bred from any Poets addle Brain.

And

And she is in the right, who tells us,

Emil. --- *A Begger in his Drink,*
Cou'd not have laid such terms upon his Callet.

This is not to describe passion. *Seneca* had another notion in the Case:

Parvæ loquuntur curæ, ingentes stupent.

And so had the Painter, who drew *Agamemnon* with his Face covered. Yet to make all worse, her Murder, and the manner of it, had before been resolv'd upon and concerted. But nothing is to provoke a Venetian; she takes all in good part; had the Scene lain in *Russia*, what cou'd we have expected more? With us a Tinkers Trull wou'd be Nettled, wou'd repartee with more spirit, and not appear so void of spleen.

Desd. *O good* Jago,
What shall I do to win my Lord agen?

No Woman bred out of a Pig-stye, cou'd talk so meanly. After this, she is call'd to Supper with *Othello, Ludovico,* &c. after that comes a filthy sort of Pastoral Scene, where the *Wedding Sheets*, and Song of *Willow*, and her Mothers Maid, poor *Barbara*, are not the least moving things in this entertainment. But that we may not be kept too long in the dumps, nor the melancholy Scenes lye too heavy, undigested on our Stomach, this *Act* gives us for a farewell, the *salsa*, *O picante*, some quibbles, and smart touches, as *Ovid* had Prophecied:

Est & in obscænos deflexa Tragœdia risus.

The last *Act* begins with *Jago* and *Roderigo*; Who a little before had been upon the huff:

Rod. *I say it is not very well: I will make my self known to* Desdemona; *if she will return me my Jewels, I will give over my suit, and repent my unlawful sollicitation, if not, assure your self, I'll seek satisfaction of you.*

Roderigo, a Noble Venetian had sought *Desdemona* in Marriage, is troubled to find the Moor had got her from him, adyises with *Jago*, who wheadles him to sell his Estate, and go over the Sea to *Cyprus*, in expectation to Cuckold *Othello*, there having

ying cheated *Roderigo* of all his Money and Jewels, on pretence of presenting them to *Desdemona*, our Gallant grows angry, and would have satisfaction from *Jago*; who sets all right, by telling him *Cassio* is to be Governour, *Othello* is going with *Desdemona* into *Mauritania*; to prevent this, you are to murder *Cassio*, and then all may be well.

Jago. *He goes into* Mauritania, *and takes with him the fair* Desdemona, *unless his abode be lingred here by some accident, wherein none can be so determinate, as the removing of* Cassio.

Had *Roderigo* been one of the *Banditi*, he might not much stick at the Murder. But why *Roderigo* should take this for payment, and risque his person where the prospect of advantage is so very uncertain and remote, no body can imagine. It had need be a *super-subtle* Venetian that this Plot will pass upon Then after a little spurt of villany and Murder, we are brought to the most lamentable, that ever appear'd on any Stage A noble Venetian Lady is to be murdered by our Poet; in sober sadness, purely for being a Fool. No Pagan Poet but wou'd

have

have found some *Machine* for her deliverance. *Pegasus* wou'd have strain'd hard to have brought old *Perseus* on his back, time enough, to rescue this *Andromeda* from so foul a Monster. Has our Christian Poetry no generosity, nor bowels? Ha, Sir *Lancelot*! ha St. *George*! will no Ghost leave the shades for us in extremity, to save a distressed Damosel?

But for our comfort, however felonious is the Heart, hear with what soft language, he does approach her, with a Candle in his Hand:

Oth. *Put out the light and then put out the light;*
If I quench thee, thou flaming Minister,
I can again thy former light restore ---

Who would call him Barbarian, Monster, Savage? Is this a Black-amoor?

Soles occidere & redire possunt ---

The very Soul and Quintessence of Sir *George Etheridge*.

One might think the General should not glory much in this action, but make an hasty work on't, and have turn'd his Eyes away from so unsouldierly
an

an Execution: yet is he all pause and deliberation; handles her as calmly: and is as careful of her Souls health, as it had been her *Father Confessor*. *Have you prayed to Night, Desdemona?* But the suspence is necessary, that he might have a convenient while so to *roul his Eyes*, and so to *gnaw his nether lip* to the spectators. Besides the greater cruelty ---*sub tam lentis maxillis*.

But hark, a most tragical thing laid to her charge.

Oth. *That Handkerchief, that I so lov'd, and gave thee,*
Thou gav'st to Cassio.

Desd. *No by my Life and Soul;*
Send for the man and ask him.

Oth. ---*By Heaven, I saw my Hankerchief in his hand --*
---*I saw the Handkerchief.*

So much ado, so much stress, so much passion and repetition about an Handkerchief! Why was not this call'd the *Tragedy of the Handkerchief?* What can be more absurd than (as *Quintilian* expresses it) *in parvis litibus has Tragœdias movere?* We have heard of *Fortunatus his Purse*, and of the *Invisible Cloak*, long ago worn threadbare,
and

and stow'd up in the Wardrobe of obsolete Romances: one might think, that were a fitter place for this Handkerchief, than that it, at this time of day, be worn on the Stage, to raise every where all this clutter and turmoil. Had it been *Desdemona*'s Garter, the Sagacious Moor might have smelt a Rat: but the Handkerchief is so remote a trifle, no Booby, on this side *Mauritania*, cou'd make any consequence from it.

We may learn here, that a Woman never loses her Tongue, even tho' after she is stifl'd.

Desd. *O falsly, falsly murder'd.*
Em. *Sweet* Desdemona, *O sweet Mistress, speak.*
Desd. *A guiltless death I dye:*
Em. *O who has done the deed?*
Desd. *No body, I my self, farewel. Commend me to my kind Lord, O farewel.*

This *Desdemona* is a black-swan; or an old Black-amoor is a bewitching Bed-fellow. If this be Nature, it is a *laschete* below what the English Language can express.

For *Lardella*, to *make love, like an Humble Bee*, was, in the Rehearsal, thought a fancy odd enough. But

But hark what follows :

Oth. ----*O heavy hour !*
Methinks it shou'd be now a huge Eclipse
Of Sun and Moon, and that the affrighted globe
Shou'd yawn at Alteration.

This is wonderful. Here is Poetry to *elevate* and *amuse*. Here is found All-sufficient. It wou'd be uncivil to ask *Flamstead*, if the Sun and Moon can both together be so hugely eclipsed, in any *heavy hour* whatsoever. Nor must the Spectators consult *Gresham* Colledge, whether a body is naturally *frighted* till he *Yawn* agen. The Fortune of *Greece* is not concern'd with these Matters. These are Physical circumstances a Poet may be ignorant in, without any harm to the publick. These slips have no influence on our Manners and good Life; which are the Poets Province.

Rather may we ask here what unnatural crime *Desdemona*, or her Parents had committed, to bring this Judgment down upon her ; to Wed a Black-amoor, and innocent to be thus cruelly murder'd by him. What instruction can we make out of this Catastrophe ? Or whtiher must our reflection

lead

lead us? Is not this to envenome and sour our spirits, to make us repine and grumble at Providence; and the government of the World? If this be our end, what boots it to be Vertuous?

Desdemona dropt the Handkerchief, and missed it that very day after her Marriage; it might have been rumpl'd up with her Wedding sheets: And this Night that she lay in her wedding sheets, the *Fairey* Napkin (whilst *Othello* was stifling her) might have started up to disarm his fury, and stop his ungracious mouth. Then might she (in a Traunce for fear) have lain as dead. Then might he, believing her dead, touch'd with remorse, have honestly cut his own Throat, by the good leave, and with the applause of all the Spectators. Who might thereupon have gone home with a quiet mind, admiring the beauty of Providence; fairly and truly represented on the Theatre.

Oth. ---*Why, how shou'd she be murdered?*
Em. Alas, who knows?
Oth. You heard her say her self it was not I.
Em. She did so, I must needs report a truth.
Oth. She's like a liar gone to burn in Hell. Twas I that did it.

Em.

Em. *O, the more Angel she
And you the blacker Devil.*

Oth. *She turn'd to folly, and she was an
Whore.*

Em. *Thou dost belye her, and thou art a
Devil.*

Oth. *She was false as Water.*

Em. *Thou art rash as Fire,
To say that she was false: O she was heavenly true.*

In this kind of Dialogue they continue for forty lines farther, before she bethinks her self, to cry Murder.

Em. --- *Help, help, O help,
The Moor has kill'd my Mistress, murder,
Murder.*

But from this Scene to the end of the Play we meet with nothing but blood and butchery, described much-what to the style of *the last Speeches and Confessions of the persons executed at Tyburn*: with this difference, that there we have the *fact*, and the due course of Justice, whereas our Poet against all Justice and Reason, against all Law, Humanity and Nature, in a barbareous arbitrary way, executes and makes

havock

havock of his subjects, *Hab-nab*, as they come to hand. *Desdemona* dropt her Handkerchief; therefore she must be stifl'd. *Othello*, by law to be broken on the Wheel, by the Poets cunning escapes with cutting his own Throat. *Cassio*, for I know not what, comes off with a broken shin. *Jago* murders his Benefactor *Roderigo*, as this were poetical gratitude. *Jago* is not yet kill'd, because there yet never was such a villain alive. The Devil, if once he brings a man to be dipt in a deadly sin, lets him alone, to take his course: and now when the *Foul Fiend* has done with him, our wise Authors take the sinner into their poetical service; there to accomplish him, and do the Devils drudgery.

Philosophy tells us it is a principle in the Nature of Man *to be grateful*.

History may tell us that *John an Oaks*, *John a Stiles*, or *Jago* were ungrateful; *Poetry* is to follow Nature; Philosophy must be his guide: history and *fact* in particular cases of *John an Oaks*, or *John a Styles*, are no warrant or direction for a Poet. Therefore *Aristotle* is always telling us that Poety is σπυδαιω]εξον ϗ φιλοσοφω]εξον, is more general and abstracted, is led more by the Philosophy, the reason and

and nature of things, than History: which only records things higlety, piglety, right or wrong as they happen. History might without any preamble or difficulty, say that *Jago* was ungrateful. Philosophy then calls him unnatural; But the Poet is not, without huge labour and preparation to expose the Monster; and after shew the Divine Vengeance executed upon him. The Poet is not to add wilful Murder to his ingratitude: he has not antidote enough for the Poison: his Hell and Furies are not punishment sufficient for one single crime, of that bulk and aggravation.

Em. *O thou dull Moor, that Handkerchief thou speakest on,*
I found by Fortune, and did give my Husband:
For often with a solemn earnestness,
(More than indeed belong'd to such a trifle)
He beg'd of me to steal it.

Here we see the meanest woman in the Play takes this *Handkerchief* for a *trifle* below her Husband to trouble his head about it. Yet we find, it entered into our Poets head, to make a Tragedy of this *Trifle*.

Then for the *unraveling of the Plot*, as they call it, never was old deputy Recorder,

der in a Country Town, with his spectacles in summoning up the evidence, at such a puzzle: so blunder'd, and be doultefied: as is our Poet, to have a good riddance: And get the *Catastrophe* off his hands.

What can remain with the Audience to carry home with them from this sort of Poetry, for their use and edification? how can it work, unless (instead of settling the mind, and purging our passions) to delude our senses, disorder our thoughts, addle our brain, pervert our affections, hair our imaginations, corrupt our appetite, and fill our head with vanity, confusion, *Tintamarre*, and Jingle-jangle, beyond what all the Parish Clarks of *London*, with their *old Testament* farces, and interludes, in *Richard* the seconds time cou'd ever pretend to? Our only hopes, for the good of their Souls, can be, that these people go to the Playhouse, as they do to Church, to sit still, look on one another, make no reflection, nor mind the Play, more than they would a Sermon.

There is in this Play, some burlesk, some humour, and ramble of Comical Wit, some shew, and some *Mimickry* to divert the spectators: but the tragical part is, plainly none other, than a Bloody Farce, without salt or savour.

CHAP.

(147)

CHAP. VIII.

Reflections on the Julius Cæsar. *Men famous in History. To be rob'd of their good name, Sacriledge.* Shakefpear, *abuse of History. Contradiction, in the character of* Brutus. Villen *and* Dantel, *that Hugh Capet from a Butcher. Preparation in Poetry. Strong reasons in* Caffius. *Roman Senators impertinent as the Venetian.* Portia *as* Defdemona. *The fame parts and good breeding. How talk of Business. Whispers.* Brutus's *Tinder-box, Sleepy Boy, Fiddle.* Brutus *and* Caffius, *Flat-foot Mimicks. The Indignity.* Laberius. *Play of the Incarnation. The* Madonna's —*Shouting and Battel. Strollers in* Cornwal. *Rehearsal, law for acting it once a week.*

The Catiline by Ben. Johnfon. *Why an Orator to be* vir bonus. Ben *cou'd distinguish Men and Manners.* Sylla's Ghoft: *The speech not to be made in a blind Corner.* Corneille. *Common fence teaches* Unity of Action. *The* Chorus, *of necessity, keep the Poet to* time, *and* place. *No rule obferv'd. A Life in* Plutarch. *Acts of the Apostles.* Ben *is* fidus interpres. *Is the Horfe in Mill in flat oppofition to* Horace. *Trifling tale, or corruption of History, unfit for Tragedy. In contempt of Poetry.* Ariftophanes, *not the occafion of the Death of* Socrates. *Was for a reformation in the fer-*

vice

vice book. *With what address he effected it.*

Sarpedon's *Fast, of divine institution. The least sally from, or Parenthesis in the ancient Comedy of more moment than all our Tragedies. English Comedy the best.*

IN the former Play, our Poet might be the bolder, the persons being all his own Creatures, and meer fiction. But here he sins not against Nature and Philosophy only, but against the most known History, and the memory of the Noblest Romans, that ought to be sacred to all Posterity. He might be familiar with *Othello* and *Jago*, as his own natural acquaintance: but *Cæsar* and *Brutus* were above his conversation. To put them in Fools Coats, and make them Jack-puddens in the *Shakespear* dress, is a *Sacriledge*, beyond any thing in *Spelman*. The Truth is, this authors head was full of villainous, unnatural images, and history has only furnish'd him with great names, thereby to recommend them to the World; by writing over them, *This is* Brutus; *this is* Cicero; *this is* Cæsar. But generally his History flies in his Face; And comes in flat contradiction to the Poets imagination. As for example: of *Brutus* says *Antony*, his Enemy.

Ant.

Ant. ----*His life was gentle, and the Elements*
So mixt in him, that Nature might stand up,
And say to all the World, this was a Man.

And when every body judg'd it necessary to kill *Antony*, our Author in his *Laconical* way, makes *Brutus* speak thus:

Bru. Our Course will seem too bloody, Caius Cassius,
To cut the Head off, and then hack the Limbs,
Like wrath in death, and envy afterwards;
For Antony *is but a Limb of* Cæsar:
Let's be Sacrificers, but not Butchers, Caius,
We all stand up against the Spirit of Cæsar,
And in the Spirit of man there is no blood;
O that we then cou'd come by Cæsars *Spirit,*
And not dismember Cæsar; *but, alas!*
Cæsar *must bleed for it. And gentle friends,*
Let's kill him boldly, but not wrathfully;
Let's carve him, as a dish fit for the Gods,
Not hew him, as a Carkass fit for Hounds.
And let our Hearts, as subtle Masters do,
Stir up their Servants to an act of rage,
And after seem to chide 'em. This shall make
Our purpose necessary, and not envious.
Which so appearing to the common eyes,

We shall be call'd Purgers, not murderers.
And for Mark Antony *think not of him:*
For he can do no more than Cæsars *arm,*
When Cæsars *head is off.*

In these two speeches we have the true character of *Brutus*, according to History. But when *Shakespear's* own blundering Maggot of self contradiction works, then must *Brutus* cry out.

Bru. ---*Stoop*, Romans, *stoop,*
And let us bath our hands in Cæsars *blood*
Up to the Elbows----

Had this been spoken by some King of France, we might remember *Villon*

Se fusse des hoirs Hue Capel,
Qui fut extrait de boucherie,
On m' eut parmy ce drapel,
Fait boire de l'escorcherie.

And what *Dante* has recorded.

Chiamato fui di là Ugo ciapetta,
Di me son Nati i Philippi, e' Loigi,
Per cui novellamente e' Francia retta,
Figlivol fui d' un Beccaio di Parigi---

For

For, indeed, that Language which *Shake-spear* puts in the Mouth of *Brutus* wou'd not suit, or be convenient, unless from some son of the Shambles, or some natural off-spring of the Butchery. But never any Poet so boldly and so barefac'd, flounced along from contradiction to contradiction. A little preparation and forecast might do well now and then. For his *Desdemona*'s Marriage, He might have helped out the probability by feigning how that some way, or other, a Black-amoor Woman had been her Nurse, and suckl'd her: Or that once, upon a time, some *Virtuoso* had transfus'd into her Veins the Blood of a black Sheep: after which she might never be at quiet till she is, as the Poet will have it, *Tupt with an old black ram.*

But to match this pithy discourse of *Brutus*; see the weighty argumentative oration, whereby *Cassius* draws him into the Conspiracy.

Cas. --- Brutus, *and* Cæsar: *what shou'd be in that* Cæsar?
Why shou'd that name be sounded more than yours?

Write

Write them together: yours is as fair a name:
Sound them, it doth become the mouth as well.
Weigh them, it is as heavy: conjure with them,
Brutus will start a Spirit as soon as Cæsar.
Now, in the names of all the Gods at once,
Upon what meat doth this our Cæsar *feed,*
That he is grown so great? Age, thou art sham'd;
Rome thou hast lost the breed of noble bloods.
When went there by an Age since the great flood,
But it was fam'd with more, than with one man?
When could they say (till now) that talk'd of Rome,
That her wide Walls encompass'd but one man?
Now it is Rome *indeed, and room enough*
When there is in it but one only Man ----

One may Note that all our Authors Senators, and his Orators had their learning and education at the same school, be they Venetians, Black-amoors, Ottamites, or noble Romans. *Brutus* and *Cassius* here, may *cap sentences*, with *Brabantio*, and the *Doge* of *Venice*, or any *Magnifico* of them all. We saw how the Venetian Senate spent their time, when, amidst their alarms, call'd to Counsel at midnight. Here the Roman
Sena-

Senators, the midnight before *Cæsar*'s death (met in the Garden of *Brutus*, to settle the matter of their Conspiracy) are gazing up to the Stars, and have no more in their heads than to wrangle about which is the East and West.

Decius. *Here lies the East, doth not the day break here?*

Caska. *Nr.*

Cinna. *O, pardon, Sir, it doth, and you grey lines,*
That fret the Clouds, are Messengers of Day.

Caska. *You shall confess, that you are both deceiv'd :*
Here as I point my Sword, the Sun arises,
Which is a great way growing on the South,
Weighing the youthful season of the year,
Some two months hence, up higher toward the North,
He first presents his fire, and the high East Stands as the Capitol directly here.

This is directly, as *Bays* tells us, *to shew the World a Pattern here, how men shou'd talk of Business.* But it wou'd be a wrong
to

to the Poet, not to inform the reader, that on the Stage, the Spectators see *Brutus* and *Cassius* all this while at *Whisper* together. That is the importance, that deserves all the attention. But the *grand question* wou'd be: does the *Audience hear 'em Whisper?*

Ush. *Why, truly I can't tell: there's much to be said upon the word Whisper*----

Another Poet wou'd have allow'd the noble *Brutus* a Watch-Candle in his Chamber this important night, rather than have puzzel'd his Man *Lucius* to grope in the dark for a Flint and Tinder-box, to get the Taper lighted. It wou'd have been no great charge to the Poet, however. Afterwards, another night, the Fiddle is in danger to be broken by this sleepy Boy.

Bru. *If thou dost nod thou break'st thy Instrument.*

But pass we to the famous Scene, where *Brutus* and *Cassius* are by the Poet represented acting the parts of *Mimicks*: from the Nobility and Buskins, they are made the *Planipedes*; are brought to daunce *barefoot*, for a Spectacle to the people, Two Philo-

Philosophers, two generals, (*imperatores* was their title) the *ultimi Romanorum*, are to play the Bullies and Buffoon, to shew their Legerdemain, their *activity* of face, and divarication of Muscles. They are to play a prize, a tryal of skill in huffing and swaggering, like two drunken Hectors, for a two-penny reckoning.

When the Roman Mettle was somewhat more allaid, and their Stomach not so very fierce, in *Augustus*'s time; *Laberius*, who was excellent at that sport, was forced once by the Emperor to shew his Talent upon the Stage: in his Prologue, he complains that

Necessity has no law.
It was the will of Cæsar *brought me hither,*
What was imagin'd for me to deny
This Cæsar; *when the Gods deny him nothing?*

But says he,

---*Ego bis tricenis annis actis sine nota,*
Eques Romanus lare egressus meo,
Domum revertor Mimus. *Nimirum hac die*
Una plus vixi mihi quam vivendum fuit---

Twice thirty years have I liv'd without blemish;
From

From home I came a Roman Gentleman,
But back shall go a Mimick. *This one day*
Is one day longer than I shou'd have liv'd.

This may shew with what indignity our Poet treats the noblest *Romans*. But there is no other cloth in his Wardrobe. Every one must be content to wear a Fools Coat, who comes to be dressed by him. Nor is he more civil to the Ladies. *Portia*, in good manners, might have challeng'd more respect : she that shines, a glory of the first magnitude in the Gallery of Heroick Dames, is with our Poet, scarce one remove from a Natural: She is the own Cousin German, of one piece, the very same impertinent silly flesh and blood with *Desdemona*. *Shakespears* genius lay for Comedy and Humour. In Tragedy he appears quite out of his Element; his Brains are turn'd, he raves and rambles, without any coherence, any spark of reason, or any rule to controul him, or set bounds to his phrenzy. His imagination was still running after his Masters, the Coblers, and Parish Clerks, and *Old Testament Stroulers*. So he might make bold with *Portia*, as they had done with the Virgin Mary. Who, in a Church Acting their Play call'd *The Incarnation*, had usually

ally the *Ave Mary* mumbl'd over to a ſtradling wench (for the bleſſed Virgin) ſtrawhatted, blew-apron'd, big-bellied, with her Immaculate Conception up to her chin.

The Italian Painters are noted for drawing the *Madonna's* by their own Wives or Miſtreſſes; one might wonder what ſort of *Betty Mackerel*, *Shakeſpear* found in his days, to fit for his *Portia*, and *Deſdemona*; and Ladies of a rank, and dignity, for their place in Tragedy. But to him a Tragedy in *Burlesk*, a merry Tragedy was no Monſter, no abſurdity, nor at all prepoſterous: all colours are the ſame to a Blind man. The Thunder and Lightning, the Shouting and Battel, and alarms every where in this play, may well keep the Audience awake; otherwiſe no Sermon wou'd be ſo ſtrong an Opiate. But ſince the memorable action by the *Putney Pikes*, the *Hammerſmith Brigate*, and the *Chelſey Cuiraſſiers*: one might think, in a modeſt Nation, no Battel wou'd ever preſume to ſhew upon the Stage agen, unleſs it were at *Perin* in *Cornwal*, where the ſtory goes that, ſome time before the year 88. the *Spaniards* once were landing to burn the Town, juſt at the nick when a Company of *Stroulers* with their

Drums

Drums and their shouting were setting *Sampson* upon the *Philistines*, which so fear'd Mr. Spaniard, that they Scampered back to their Galions, as apprehending our whole *Tilbury* Camp had lain in Ambush, and were coming souse upon them.

At *Athens* (they tell us) the Tragedies of *Æsculus*, *Sophocles*, and *Euripides* were enroll'd with their Laws, and made part of their Statute-Book.

We want a law for Acting the *Rehearsal* once a week, to keep us in our senses, and secure us against the Noise and Nonsence, the Farce and Fustian which, in the name of Tragedy, have so long invaded, and usurp our Theater.

Tully defines an Orator to be, *Vir bonus dicendique peritus*. Why must he be a *good Man*, as if a bad Man might not be a good Speaker? But what avails it to Speak well, unless a man is well heard? To gain attention *Aristotle* told us, it was necessary that an Orator be a *good Man*; therefore he that writes Tragedy should be careful that the persons of his *Drama*, be of consideration and importance, that the Audience may readily lend an Ear, and give attention to what they say, and act. Who would thrust into a crowd a crowd to hear what Mr. *Jago, Roderigo,* or *Cassio,* is like to say? From a Venetian Senate, or a Roman Senate one might expect great matters: But their Poet was out of sorts; he had it not for them; the Senators must be no wiser than other folk.

Ben. Johnson, knew to distinguish men and manners, at an other rate. In *Catiline* we find our selves in *Europe,* we are no longer in the *Land of Savages,* amongst Blackamoors, Barbarians, and Monsters.

The Scene is Rome and first on the Stage appears *Sylla's* Ghost.

Dost thou not feel me, Rome? Not yet?

One would, in reason, imagine the Ghost is in some publick open place, upon some Eminence, where Rome is all within his view: But it is a surprizing thing to find that this ratling Rodomontado speech is in a dark, close, private sleeping hole of *Catiline's,*

Yet the *Chorus,* is of all wonders the strangest. The *Chorus* is always present on the Stage, privy to, and interessed in all that passes,

passes, and thereupon make their Reflections to Conclude the several *Acts*.

Sylla's Ghost, tho' never so big, might slide in at the Key-hole; but how comes the *Chorus* into *Catilins* Cabinet?

Aurelia is soon after with him too, but the Poet had perhaps provided her some Truckle-bed in a dark Closet by him.

In short, it is strange that *Ben*, who understood the turn of Comedy so well; and had found the success, should thus grope in the dark, and jumble things together without head or tail, without any rule or proportion, without any reason or design. Might not the *Acts of the Apostles*, or a Life in *Plutarch*, be as well Acted, and as properly called a Tragedy, as any History of a Conspiracy?

Corneille tells us, in the *Examen* of his *Melite*, that when first he began to write, he thought there had been no Rules: So had no guide but a little *Common sence*, with the Example of Mr. *Hardy*, and some others, not more regular than he. This *Common sence* (says he) *which was all my rule*

rule, *brought me to find out the unity of Action to imbroyl four Lovers by one and the same intreague.* Ben. *Johnson*, besides his Common sence to tell him that the *Unity of Action* was necessary; had stumbl'd (I know not how) on a *Chorus*; which is not to le drawn through a Key-hole, to be lugg'd about, or juggl'd with an *hocus pocus* hither and thither; nor stow'd in a garret, nor put into quarters with the *Breentford* Army, so must of necessity keep the Poet to *unity of place*; And also to some Conscionable *time*, for the representation: Because the *Chorus* is not to be trusted out of sight, is not to eat or drink till they have given up their Verdict, and the *Plaudite* is over.

One would not talk of rules, or what is regular with *Shakespear*, or any followers, in the Gang of the *Strouling* Fraternity; but it is lamentable that *Ben. Johnson*, his Stone and his Tymber, however otherwise of value, must lye a miserable heap of ruins, for want of Architecture, or some Son of *Vitruvius*, to joyn them together. He had red *Horace*, had Translated that to the *Pisones*:

M   *Nec*

Nec verbum verbo curabis reddere, fidus interpres.----

Ben. ----*Being a Poet, thou may'st feign,*
(create,
Not care, as thou wouldst faithfully tran-
(slate,

To render word for word---

And this other precept.

Nec circa vilem, patulumque morabe is Orbem.

Ben. --*The vile, broad-trodden ring for-*
sake.

What is there material in this *Catiline*, either in the *Manners*, in the *Thoughts*, or in the *Expression*, (three parts of Tragedy) which is not word for word tranflation? In the *Fable*, or Plot (which is the firft, and principal part) what fee we, but the *vile broad trodden ring*? *Vile*, *Horace* calls it, as a thing below, and too mean for any man of wit to bufie his head withal. *Patulum*, he calls it, becaufe it is obvious,
and

and eafie for any body to do as much as that comes to. 'Tis but to plodd along, ftep by ftep in the fame tract : 'Tis drudgery only for the blind Horfe in a Mill. No Creature found of Wind and Limb, but wou'd chufe a nobler Field, and a more generous Career.

Homer, we find, flips fometime into a *Tract* of *Scripture*, but his *Pegafus* is not ftabl'd there, prefently up he fprings, mounts aloft, is on the wing, no earthly bounds, or barriers to confine him.

For *Ben*, to fin thus againft the cleareft light and conviction, argues a ftrange ftupidity: It was bad enough in him, againft his Judgment and Confcience, to interlard fo much fiddle-faddle, Comedy, and *Apocryphal* matters in the Hiftory : Becaufe, forfooth,

---*his nam plebecula gaudet*.

Where the Poet has chofen a fubject of importance fufficient and proper for Tragedy, there is no room for this petty interlude and diverfion. Had fome Princes come exprefs from *Salankemen* (remote as it is)

to give an account of the battel, whilft the ftory was hot and new, and made a relation accurate, and diftinctly, with all the pomp, and advantage of the Theatre, wou'd the Audience have fuffer'd a Tumbler or Baboon, a Bear, or Rope dancer to have withdrawn their attention; or to have interrupted the Narrative; tho' it had held as long as a Dramatick Reprefentation. Nor at that time wou'd they thank a body for his quibbles, or wit out of feafon: This mans Feather, or that Captains Embroidered Coat might not be touched upon but in a very fhort *Parenthefis*.

It is meerly by the ill-chofen Subject, or the ill-adjufting it, that the Audience runs a gadding after what is forreign, and from the bufinefs. And when fome fencelefs trifling tale, as that of *Othello*; or fome mangl'd, abus'd, undigefted, interlarded Hiftory on our Stage impioufly affumes the facred name of Tragedy, it is no wonder if the Theatre grow corrupt and fcandalous, and Poetry from its Ancient Reputation and Dignity, is funk to the utmoft Contempt and Derifion.

Many have been offended with *Ariftophanes*

nes as accessary to the death of *Socrates* ; but who so shall consider the State of affairs at that juncture, when *the Clouds* was acted, might sooner believe the Poets design was rather *previous*, (as we call it) to try the strength of a Party, by the Countenance of the People : And the success of this Play, they discovered how far the interest of *Alcibiades* prevailed. *Alcibiades* was the dangerous man to the Government, too big for the Republick, and for *Aristophanes* himself.

Socrates came not to be judicially arraigned in twenty years after the Comedy. They first had made sure of his protector, and got him out of the way. Upon which, the Common-wealth party took heart, and wou'd make the Philosopher answer for the rare accomplishments which *Alcibiades* had drawn from him, and so ill Employed.

Socrates should not have mocked at the *Old Religion*, till sure of some means to introduce a better. *Socrates* had not the gift of Miracles.

Alcibiades with his Companions cou'd learn from *Socrates* to blaspheme the established Worſhip: But were too ſenſual for a urer Faith, and Divine ſpeculations.

Thereupon followed ſo many mad pranks amongſt them: As that for example, when the Gods of the Town (ſet at every mans Door) were, as they had been ſo many Sign-poſts, all in one night broken down. How would the People look, after this outrage? What cou'd they expect, but Hell to ſwallow 'em up all quick, the next morning?

Ariſtophanes, in a ſober way, was not aga'nſt a Reformation. He attempted an alteration, and wrought it Effectually. As particularly: The *Athenians*, wanting a true Calculation of the courſe of the Moon, were often in great confuſion about their Holy-days. They kept Faſt often when they ſhould have Feaſted, and other times had their Feſtival on a work-day; and many times the Feaſt and Faſt came a-pick a-pack. To rectifie this, in that very Play (*the Clouds*) againſt *Socrates*, there the *Chorus* returns, and addreſſes to the Spectators, in this manner.

As we were departing, the Moon *(our Lady) met us,*
And bid us tell ye, Firſt,

First, that *she* gives her love to *you*, and your *Confederates*.

In the next place that *she* is angry with *you*, as *ill* dealt withal by *you*,

For her good turns to all of *you*, not in words,

but *Effectually*.

In particular, every month *She* saves you two pence half-penny, in *Lanthorn* and *Candle-Light* :

And then going abroad a nights you cry, *Hold, boy, there needs no Link, 'tis Moon-shine.*

In other respects She likes you well,

Saving that you are out in your *Accounts* most shamefully.

Jumbling all things hand over head counfounedly ;

In so much that the *Gods* threaten her immoderately :

When their appetite is baulk'd, and they go home with hungry *Nostrils*, because you want a good *Almanac*.

For when you should be *Sacrificing*,

Then are you at the *Sessions*, trying *Felons* and *Pick-pockets*.

On the other hand, when 'tis *Ember-week* in *Heaven*,

And all are *Fasting*, with an *a-lack* ; and well a day :

For the death of Memnon *or* **Sarpedon ;**
Then smoak your Hecatombs---

By this, every body were convinced that the *form* by law established wanted amendment; the Priests from all parts were gather'd together? they were asham'd of their Calendar, Reform, Reform was the only cry amongst 'em; Not one *Nolumus*---In all the Convocation.

And thereupon *Meton*, the Mathematician was sent for, and set to work; And from thence our Chrono-graphers had a new *Epocha*.

From this place we may observe another reason for *Homer*, against the * objection by *Plato*, to wit, that *Homer* had an eye to the Greek *Liturgie*, And that passage in *Homer* was to show *Sarpedons Fast* to be of *Divine Institution*.

This small Sally, or start out from the play, is of greater Moment, is of more weight and importance, than all the Tragedies on our Stage con'd pretend to. And yet for modern Comedy, doubtless our English are the best in the World.

* vid page 34.

Extrait

Extrait des Regiſtres du Parlement du Vendredy, 9. Decembre l'an 1541. *Monſieur de S. André Preſident.*

ENtre le Procureur General du Roy prenant le fait en main pour les pauvres de Paris demandeur & requerant l enterinement d'une Requeſte par luy preſentée à la Cour, d'une part,

Et Maiſtre François Hamelin Notaire au Chaſtelet de Paris, François Pouldrain, Leonard Choblets, Jean Louvet, Maiſtres Entrepreneurs du Jeu, & Myſtere des Actes des Apoſtres, n'agueres executé en cette Ville de Paris, défendeurs à l'enterinement de ladite Requeſte, d'autre.

Le Maiſtre pour le Procureur du Roy, dit qu'anciennement les Romains inſtituerent pluſieurs jeux publics, de la plus part deſquels parle Tite Live, & les recite tous Flavius qui a écrit *de Roma triumphante*. Mais quelques jeux que ce fuſſent, il n'y en avoit aucuns qui fuſſent ordinaires ; ains ne ſe faiſoient ſinon les occaſions occurrentes, & pour quelques cauſes notables & inſignes,
comme

comme pour quelque victoire ou triomphe, ou pour quelque pompe funebre ou autre notable cause. Vray est que Festus Pompeïus recite une maniere de jeux qui se faisoient sans occasions, *& dicebantur ludi sæculares* ; mais ils ne se faisoient, *nisi centesimo quoque anno*. Et encore apres que les Romains furent attediez de tels jeux publics & qu'ils connurent qu'ls tournoient en lasciveté, *& in perniciem* de la Republique, ils les laisserent : & y eut loy expresse que les frais & impenses qui se faisoient de jeux publics, seroient employez és reparations de la ville de Rome: Et encore est aujourd'huy cette loy écrite, *l. unica c. de Expensis ludorum lib.* 11.

Et pour le fait, dit que puis trois ou quatre ans en ca les Maistres dela Passion ont entrepris de faire joüer & representer le Mystere de la Passion qui a esté fait, & parce qu'il s'est trouvé qu'ils y ont fait gros gain, sont venus aucuns particuliers gen non lettrez, ny entendus en telles affaires, & gens de condition infame, comme un Menusier, un Sergent à Verge, & un Tapissier & autres qui ont fait joüer les Actes des Apostres, en iceux commis plusieurs fautes, tant aux feintes qu'au jeu, & pour allonger le temps on fait composer, dicter & adjouster plusieurs fieurs chofes apocryphes, quoy que foit non contenuës és Actes des Apoftres, & fait durer trois ou quatre journées, afin d'exiger plus d'argent du peuple, en entremettant à la fin ou au commencement du jeu, farces lafcives & de mocqueries, en ont fait durer leur jeu l'efpace de fix ou fept mois, d'où font advenus, & adviennent ceffations de fervice divin, refroidiffement de charitez & aumofnes, adulteres & fornications infinies, fcandales, derifions & mocqueries.

Et pour les declarer en premier lieu par le menu, dit que pendant lefdits jeux, & tant qu'il ont duré, le commun peuple dés huit à neuf heures du matin és jours de Feftes delaiffoit fa Meffe Paroiffiale, Sermon & Vefpres pour aller efdits jeux garder fa place, & y eftre jufqu'à cinq heures du foir : ont ceffé les Predications, car n'euffent eu les Predicateurs qui les euft écoutez. Et retournant defdits jeux, fe mocquoient hautement & publiquement par les ruës defdits jeux & des joüeurs, contrefaifant quelque langage impropre qu'ils avoient ouy defdits jeux ou autre chofe mal faite, criant par derifion que le S. Efprit n'avoit point voulu defcendre, & par d'autres mocqueries. Et le plus fouvent les Preftres des
Paroiffes

Paroisses pour avoir leur passe-temps d'aller esdits jeux, ont delaissé dire Vespres les jours de Festes, ou les ont dites tout seuls dés l'heure de Midy, heure non accoustumée: & mesme les Chantres ou Chappellains de la Sainte Chappelle de ce Palais tant que lesdits jeux ont duré, ont dit Vespres les jours de Festes à l'heure de midy, & encore les disoient en poste & à la legere pour aller esdits jeux, chose indecente, non accoustumée & de mauvais exemple, & contre les saints Conciles de l'Eglise, mesme contre le Concile de Chartage, *in c. qui die de consecrat. dist.* 1. où est dit: *Qui die solemni prætermisso Ecclesiæ conventu ad Spectacula vadit, excommunicetur.*

Secundò, les Predications sont plus decentes pour l'instruction du peuple, attendu qu'elles se font par Theologiens gens doctes & de sçavoir, que ne sont les Actes ou representations qu'on appelle jeux que font gens ignorans & indoctes qui n'entendent ce qu'ils font ne ce qu'ils dient, representant les Actes des Apostres, le vieux Testament & autres semblables Histoires qu'ils s'efforcent de representer.

Tertiò, il est certain & indubitable par jugement

jugement natural que fiction d'une chose n'eſt poſſible ſans prealable intelligence de la verité. Car fiction n'eſt autre choſe qu'une approche que l'ons s'efforce faire au plus prez que l'on peut de la verité. Et tant les Entrepreneurs que les joüeurs ſont gens ignares & non lettrez qui ne ſcavent ny A. ny B. qui n'ont intelligence non ſeulement de la Sainte Ecriture, *immò* ny d'Ecritures prophanes. Sont les joüeurs artiſans mechaniques, comme Cordonniers, Savetiers, Crocheteurs de Greve, de tous eſtats & arts mechaniques, qui ne ſcavent lire ny ecrire, & qui on-ques ne furent inſtruits ny exercez en Theatres & lieux publics à faire tels actes, & davantage n'ont langue diſerte ny langage propre, ny les accens de prononciation decente, ny aucune intelligence de ce qu'ils dient : tellement que le plus ſouvent advient que d'un mot ils en font trois : font point ou pauſe au milieu d'une propoſition, ſens ou oraiſon imparfaite ; font d'un interrogant un admirant, ou autre geſte, prolation au accent contraires à ce qu'ils dient, dont ſouvent advient deriſion & clameur publique dedans le Theatre meſme, tellement qu'au lieu de tourner à édification, leur jeu tourne à ſcandale & deriſion.

Quartò,

Quartò, ils meſlent le plus ſouvent des farces, & autres jeux impudiques, laſcifs ou deriſoires qu'ils jouënt à la fin ou au commencement, pour attirer le commun peuple à y retourner, qui ne demande que telles voluptez & folies, qui ſont choſes défenduës par tous les Saints Conciles de l'Egliſe, de meſler Farces & Comedies deriſoires avec les Myſteres Eccleſiaſtiques, ainſi qu'il eſt traitté par tous les Doƈteurs *in c. cum decorem. de vita & honeſtate Clericorum, & per hoc in ſumma eodem titulo. Item ludi Theatrales.* Et par le Concile de Baſle au decret *de Speƈtaculis in Eccleſia non faciendis.*

Quintò, l'on reconnoiſt oculairement que tout ce qu'ils en font, eſt ſeulement pour le queſt & pour le gain, comme ils feroient d'une Taverne ou negotiation, & qu'ils veulent devenir Hiſtrions, Joculateurs ou Batteleurs; car comme dit Panorm. *in tit. cum decorem,* un perſonnage eſt reputé Hiſtrion, Batteleur & Joculateur quand par deux fois il retourne *cauſa queſtus* à faire jeux ou ſpeƈtacles publics... & ainſi en propres termes le declare Panorm. *in diƈto tit. cum decorem.* C'y l'on void que ja par deux fois

fois il y font venus pour le queſt & profit feulement, & d'an en an, ils hauſſent le prix; car la premiere année ils faiſoient payer vingt & cinq eſcus pour chacune loge, & la ſeconde ils en ont fait payer trente & trente ſix eſcus; & maintenant ils les mettent à quarente & cinquante eſcus ſol. Ainſi l'on connoiſt oculairement qu'il n'y a que le queſt & profit particulier qui les mene, & ne font qu'inventions pour tirer ſubtilement argent du peuple.

Sextò, il advient mille inconveniens & maux; car ſous couleur de ces jeux, ſe font pluſieurs parties & aſſignations, infinies fornications, adulteres, maquerellages. Et pour cette cauſe eſt *eadem rubrica jeu titulus in lib.* 11. *c. de Spectaculis, & Scenicis, & Lenonibus.*

Septimò, ſi font eſdits jeux commeſſations & dépenſes extraordinaires par le commun peuple; tellement que ce qu'un pauvre artiſan aura gagné toute la ſemaine, il l'ira dépendre en un jour eſdits jeux, tant pour payer à l'entrée, qu'en commeſſation & yvrogneſſe; & faudra que ſa femme & enfans en endurent toute la ſemain.

Octavò,

Octavo, l'on a connu par experience que lesdits jeux ont grandement diminué les charitez & aufmofnes, tellement qu'en fix mois qu'ont duré lefdits jeux, les aufmones ont diminué de la fomme de trois mille livres, & en appert par certification fignée des Commiffaires fur le fait des pauvres.

Ce neanmoins un nommé le Royer, & vendeur de poiffon, un Tapiffier, un Menufier & quelues autres leurs compagnons ont de nouveau entrepris de faire jouër l'année prochane le vieil Teftament, & veulent faire deformais un ordinaire defdits jeux pour exiger argent du peuple.

Dont averty le Procureur General du Roy, a prefenté fa Requefte pour leur faire inhibitions & défenfes de non paffer outre à leur entreprife. Ils luy ont apporté une lettre de Privilege qu'ils difent avoir obtenu du Roy, qu'ils ont prefentée avec une Requefte au Lieutenant Criminel qui ne leur a voulu repondre. Au moyen de quoy ils fe font retirez au Lieutenant Civil, qui leur a repondu leur Requefte, & pour ce que par lefdites lettres ils ont donné à entendre au Roy qu'ils le font par zele de devotion,

&

(177)

& pour l'édification du peuple, qui eft chofe non veritable, & y repugne leur qualité & encore plus leurs facultez : mais le font feulement par une negotiation ou marchandife & pour le queft, gain & profit qu'ils en efperent, & autrement ne le feroient. Davantage y a plufieus chofes au Vieil Teftament qu'il n'eft expedient declarer au peuple, comme gens ignorance & imbecilles, qui pourroit prendre occafion de Judaïfme à faute d'intelligence.

Pour ces caufes & autres confiderations qui feroient de long recit, conclud à l'enterinement de fa Requefte ; & en ce faifant que défenfes leur foient faites de non paffer outre à leur entreprife defdits Jeux du vieil Teftament, jufqu'au bon plaifir, vouloir & intention du Roy, les chofes fufdites par luy entenduës.

A auffi ledit Procureur General prefenté autre Requefte, à ce que pour les caufes fufdites, les anciens Entrepreneurs foient tenus mettre, & delivrer de leur gain & deniers procedans defdits jeux des Actes des Apoftres, la fomme de huit cens livres parifis en la boëte aux pauvres par provifion, & fauf apres avoir veu par la Cour l'eftat de leurs frais & de leur gain, en ordonner plus grande fomme, fi faire fe doit. Ainfi en fut

fut en pareil cas ordonné contre les Maiſtres de la Paſſion. Et requiert qu'à ce faire ils ſoient contraints chacun de eux ſeul, & pour le tout, par vente & exploitation de leurs biens, & meſme par empriſonnement de leurs perſonnes, & conclud.

Ryant dit qu'il n'a charge de défendre a la Requeſte du Procureur General du Roy pour le regard des Maiſtres Entrepreneurs du myſtere des Actes des Apoſtres ; mais ſeulement à charge pour les nouveaux Maiſtres Entrepreneurs du myſtere de l'ancien Teſtament, remontre à la Cour les cauſes qui les ont meus à entreprendre faire executer le myſtere de l'ancien Teſtament. Eſt que le Roy ayant veu jouër quelque fois le myſtere de la Paſſion y a deux ans, & pour le rapport qui luy a eſté fait de l'execution du myſtere des Actes des Apoſtres, & averty qu'il ſeroit bon voir la repreſentation de l'ancien Teſtament, un nommé le Royer s'eſtoit retiré vers luy, & luy auroit donné à entendre, que ſous ſon bon plaiſir il entreprendroit volontiers à faire repreſenter cet ancien Teſtament par myſtere: à quoy volontiers le Roy avoit incliné, tellement qu'il avoit permis audit le Royer faire repreſenter ledit ancien Teſtament par myſtere; & à cette cauſe luy avoit fait expedier ſes lettres patentes addreſdreffantes au Prevoſt de Paris Juge ordinaire. Le Royer ayant lefdites lettres, en demande en Chaſtelet la verification appellez les gens du Roy. De leur confentement ledit Prevoſt de Paris ou fon Lieutenant en enterinant lefdites lettres, permit audit le Royer qu'il commence à faire faire quelques preparatifs pour l'execution. Et connoiffant que luy feul ne pouvoit fubvenir aux frais neceffaires pour la grandeur de l'acte & magnificence qu'il y falloit garder, affocie avec luy quatre ou cinq honneſtes Marchans de cette ville. Et pour autant que tous eſtoient ignorans des frais que l'on pourroit faire, prennent avec eux un des Maiſtres entrepreneurs des Actes des Apoſtres pour les inſtruire de ce qui leur conviendroit faire. Et eux fe penfant affeurez au moyen de la permiffion du Roy, & de la verification faite du confentement des Gens du Roy, marchandent aux Marchands de Draps de foye & autres pour les fournir des étofes qu'il leur falloit ; & ont avance grande fomme de deniers, aux uns deux mille livres, aux autres fept cens, tellement qu'il y a obligation fur eux de plus de fept mille livres. Ont fait dreffer le livre de l'ancien Teſtament, iceluy communiqué au Theologien Picard pour oſter ce qu'il verroit ne'ſtre à dire : Ont choiſi gens experts

& entendus pour executer le myftere. Et font quafi tous les roolles faits, & ja par tout publiez que l'on doit jouër. Neantmoins le Procureur General du Roy par une Requefte prefentée à la Cour les avoit inhibé de paffer outre. Dit qu'ils ne veulent eftre defobeiffans à la Cour ; mais attendu les Lettres Patentes du Roy, la verification du confentement des Gens du Roy, la Cour fous correction, doit lever les défenfes. Joint qu'il n'eft queftion de *ludis pertinentibus tantum ad ornatum urbis, vel lætitiam populi*, qui encore ne feroient prohibez ; mais de l'édification du peuple en noftre foy. Il eft vray que les Entrepreneurs ne font gens pour faire l'edification ; mais que par l'Hiftoire joüée fera reprefenté l'Ancien Teftament ; & le pourront les rudes, & non fcavans mieux comprendre à le voir à l'œil, que par la feule parole qui en pourroit eftre faite. Et de dire qu'il y a des fcandales, & des affemblées mauvaifes, & que les aumofnes des pauvres en pourront eftre refroidies ; cela n'eft confiderable ; car ne s'eft point trouvé qu'il y ait eu de fcandales, ny mauvaifes affemblées aux myfteres de la Paffion, & Actes des Apoftres. Et quant aux aumofnes elles fe refroidiffent tous les jours pour autre caufe que chacun ne fcait pas. A cette caufe fupplie la Cour, veu la permiffion mission du Roy, la verification d'icelle; & consideré les preparatifs que les Entrepreneurs ont faits, & que *res non est amplius integra*, il plaise à la Cour lever lesdites défenses, autrement perdroient les pauvres gens beaucoup. Et neanmoins offre du gain qu'ils pourront faire que la Cour en ordonne telle somme qu'elle verra pour les pauvres.

Le Maistre dit qui'l n'y a point permission du Prevost de Paris ; ains au contraire ledit Prevost a ordonné qu'aucuns seroient appellez, pour ouyr aprés òrdonner ce que de raison.

A dit Ryant que s'y est : a leu la Requeste presentée audit Prevost, réponduë, & signée De Mesme.

A dit le Maistre qu'il y avoit objection : Car premierement s'estoient addressez au Lieutenant Criminel qui les avoit refusez. Et pour ce requiert les défenses tenir jusques à ce que le Procureur General aura adverty le Roy ; & que sur ce il aura entendu son intention, & vouloir.

Interpellé Ryant s'il vouloit rien dire pour les Maistres des Actes des Apostres, a dit qu'il y en a un, ou deux presens, qui luy font dire quils sont prests de rendre compte.

La Cour dit qu'en ayant égard à la requeste faite par ledit Procureur General du Roy,

Roy, elle a ordonné, & ordonne que les Anciens Maiſtres bailleront la ſomme de 800. liv. pariſis par proviſion, pour employer à l'aliment & nourriture des pauvres de cette Ville de Paris : & ſemblablement mettront pardevers ladite Cour leur eſtat, & compte ; pour iceluy veu leur eſtre pourveu ainſi qu'il appartiendra par raiſon: & à ce faire ils feront contraints par priſe de corps, un ſeul pour le tour. Et quant à la ſeconde requeſte dudit Procureur General, tendant à ce que défenſes fuſſent faites aux nouveaux Maiſtres Entrepreneurs du myſtere de l'Ancien Teſtament, ladite Cour a fait & fait inhibitions & défenſes auſdits nouveaux Maiſtres de proceder à l'execution de leur entrepriſe, juſqu'à ce qu'elle ait ſceu ſur ce le bon plaiſir & vouloir du Roy, pour iceluy ouy, leur faire telle permiſſion, qu'il plaira audit Seigneur ordonner.

Aprés lequel prononcé a requis Ryant delay eſtre donné auſdits Maiſtres Anciens pour bailler ladite ſomme de huit cens livers car ils n'avoient *præſentem pecuniam*.

A dit Brulart Procureur General qu'il leu raccorde quinzaine. Ladite Cour a ordonné que leſdits Anciens Maiſtres payeront la moitié de ladite ſomme dedans quinzaine, & l'autre moitié la quinzaine enſuivant.

FINIS.

A Catalogue of Books, Printed for Richard Baldwin.

State Tracts; being a further Collection of several Choice Treatises relating to the Government, from the year 1660 to 1689. Now published in a Body, to shew the Necessity and clear the Legality of the late Revolution, and our present happy Settlement, under the auspicious Reign of Their Majesties King *William* and Queen *Mary*.

A Brief Disquisition of the Law of Nature, according to the Principles and Method laid down in the Reverend Dr. *Comberlands* (now Lord Bishop of *Peterborough*) Latin Treatise on that Subject. As also his confutation of Mr. *Hobbs*'s Principles put into another method, with the Right Reverend Authors approbation.

Bibliotheca Politica: Or, a Discourse by way of Dialogue, whether the *Commons* of *England* represented by *Knights, Citizens* and *Burgesses* in *Parliament*, weere one of the Three *Estates in Parliament* before the 49th of *Henry* III. or 18th of *Edw.* I. Collected out of the most approved Authors, both Ancient and Modern. Dialogue the Sixth.

Mercurius Reformatus: Or the New Observator. Containing Reflections upon the most Remarkable Events falling out from time to time in *Europe*, and more particularly in *England*. The Fifth Volume, Printed for *Rich. Baldwin*; where are also to be had the *First, Second, Third,* and *Fourth Volumes*, with the *Appendix* to them.

The Speech of the Right honourable *Thomas* Earl of *Stamford*, Lord *Gray* of *Grooby*, &c. at the General Quarter-Sessions held for the County of *Leicester*, at Michaelmas, 1691. His Lordship being made *Custos Rotulorum* for the said County, by the late Lord Commissioners of the Great Seal.

Truth brought to Light; or the History of the first 14 years of King *James* I. In Four Parts. I. The happy state of *England* at his Majesty's Entrance; the corruption of it afterwards. With the Rise of Particular Favourites, and the Divisions between

tween this and other States abroad. II. The Divorce betwixt the Lady *Francis Howard*, and *Robert* Earl of *Essex*, before the King's Delegates, authorized under the King's Broad-Seal: As also the Arraignment of Sir *Jer. Ellis*, Lieutenant of the *Tower, &c.* about the murther of Sir *Tho. Overbury*, with all Proceedings thereupon, and the King's gracious Pardon and Favour to the Countess. III. A Declaration of his Majesty's Revenue since he came to the Crown of *England*; with the Annual Issues, Gifts, Pensions, and extraordinary Disbursements. IV. The Commissions and Warrants for the burning of two Hereticks, newly revived, with two Pardons, one for *Theophilus Higgons*, the other for Sir *Eustace Hart*.

A Poem, occasioned by the late Discontents and Disturbances in the State. With Reflections upon the Rise and Progress of Priest-Craft. Written by *N. Tate*.

The *Folly* of *Priest-Craft*, a Comedy.

The Memoirs of Monsieur *Deageant*; containing the most secret Transactions and Affairs, from the Death of *Henry* IV. till the beginning of the Ministry of the Cardinal *de Richelieu*. To which is added, a particular Relation of the Arch-bishop of *Embrun*'s Voyage into *England*, and of his Negotiation for the Advancement of the Roman Catholick Religion here; together with the Duke of *Buckingham's* Letters to the said Arch-Bishop, about the progress of that Affair; which happen'd the last Years of King *James* I. his Reign. Faithfully translated out of the *French* Original.

The Cabinet Open'd; or, the Secret History of the Amours of Madam *de Maintenon* with the *French* King. Translated from the *French* Copy.

Europe's Chains broke; or a sure and speedy Project to Rescue Her from the present Usurpations of the Tyrant of *France*.

A True Relation of the Cruelties and Barbarities of the *French*, upon the *English* Prisoners of War. Being a Journal of their Travels from *Dinan* in *Brittany*, to *Thoulon* in *Provence* and back again. With a Description of the Scituation, and Fortifications of all the Eminent Towns upon the Road, and their Distance. Of their Prisons and Hospitals, and the number of Men that died under their Cruelty: With the Names of many of them, and the places of their Deaths and Burials: With an Account of the great Charity and sufferings of the poor Protestants of *France*; And other material Things that happened upon the Way.

FINIS.